HOPE *worldwide* Centers of Excellence ESOL Book 1
Student Edition

Copyright © 2015 by HOPE *worldwide* Ltd.

All rights reserved. This book or any portion thereof may not be reproduced or used in any manner whatsoever without the express written permission of the HOPE *worldwide* Ltd. except for the use of brief quotations in a book review.

Printed in the United States of America
First Printing, 2015

ISBN-13: 978-0692839584
ISBN-10: 0692839585

HOPE *worldwide* Centers of Excellence
4231 Balboa Avenue #330
San Diego, CA 92117

HOPE *worldwide* Centers of Excellence ESOL Book 1
Student Edition

ACKNOWLEDGEMENTS

The author and publisher are very grateful to those who have cooperated in different ways to the production of this material.

We are deeply grateful to Free Bible Images and Sweet Publishing for given us permission to use their Bible images.

The publisher and author are grateful to all those who have provided information, personal stories, and/or photographs.

We are very grateful to the numerous individuals who cooperated in recording the audios for the lessons.

We are indebted to those who edited the book and provided detailed feedback and suggestions for the book.

We are grateful with those who participated in different areas of the production of the first edition of the book.

We are truly grateful to the people who made the development and printing of the book possible; the HOPE worldwide team, and the many donors and friends in the United States who gave generously of their time, energy, and their personal resources.

A NOTE FROM THE AUTHOR
Jeannette Aracely Borjas Cáceres

I am truly grateful to God for the opportunity to develop this English program. I want to thank my family, my dear husband J and my beloved children, for all their support, encouragement and inspiration.

To God be the glory!

TO THE STUDENT

Dear Student,

Welcome to our ESOL Program!

This curriculum has been designed and written specifically with your needs in mind first and foremost. I am convinced that God has made this possible. The ESOL program started as a dream to help you learn English in order to have better life opportunities. We want you to be able to learn English and also grow in your love for God, through a series of Bible verses and stories that will teach you God's word and will encourage you to practice moral values in your daily life. Bible stories are related with each thematic lesson, providing you examples of vocabulary or grammar usage in real life context.

This is a communicative course, which will help you to acquire the language in a practical, natural way. In order to do so, it provides enough oral practice for you to communicate successfully in English. It also provides practice in all four communication skills, with a special focus on listening and speaking. This phonics–based curriculum from units one to six, is designed for students beginning at level zero.

The curriculum includes a variety of exercises considering the different learning styles our students might have. It contains oral practice, reading practice and comprehension exercises, as well as dictations of words and sentences, writing exercises and special exercises to 'talk about' the topics learned in each lesson. Vocabulary is build up in each lesson and presented through illustrations to provide you a visual aid of the new word.

Each topic in the curriculum includes an 'at home' lesson that offers the written practice of new functions and structures. It includes an exercise of each topic learned in class, as well as different activities to be done at home to reinforce the learning of English. In order to achieve your learning goals sooner, we encourage you to study at home, submerge yourself in the English language by reading as much as possible, listening to the audios, listening to music, and above all, challenge yourself to practice what you learn.

This program includes a CD which provides you with the audio of the new vocabulary, phonetic sounds, Bible Scriptures or stories, dialogues and conversations. We personalized the book for students by using our students' photographs to illustrate the different series of the book as well as some of our students' stories, biographies, and real experiences, which serve as reading and conversational material for the lessons.
Finally, you will find some tips that can help you speed the learning process. You will see how learning English will open a wide range of opportunities in your life. I hope you enjoy learning!

Jeannette Borjas

ESOL PROGRAM

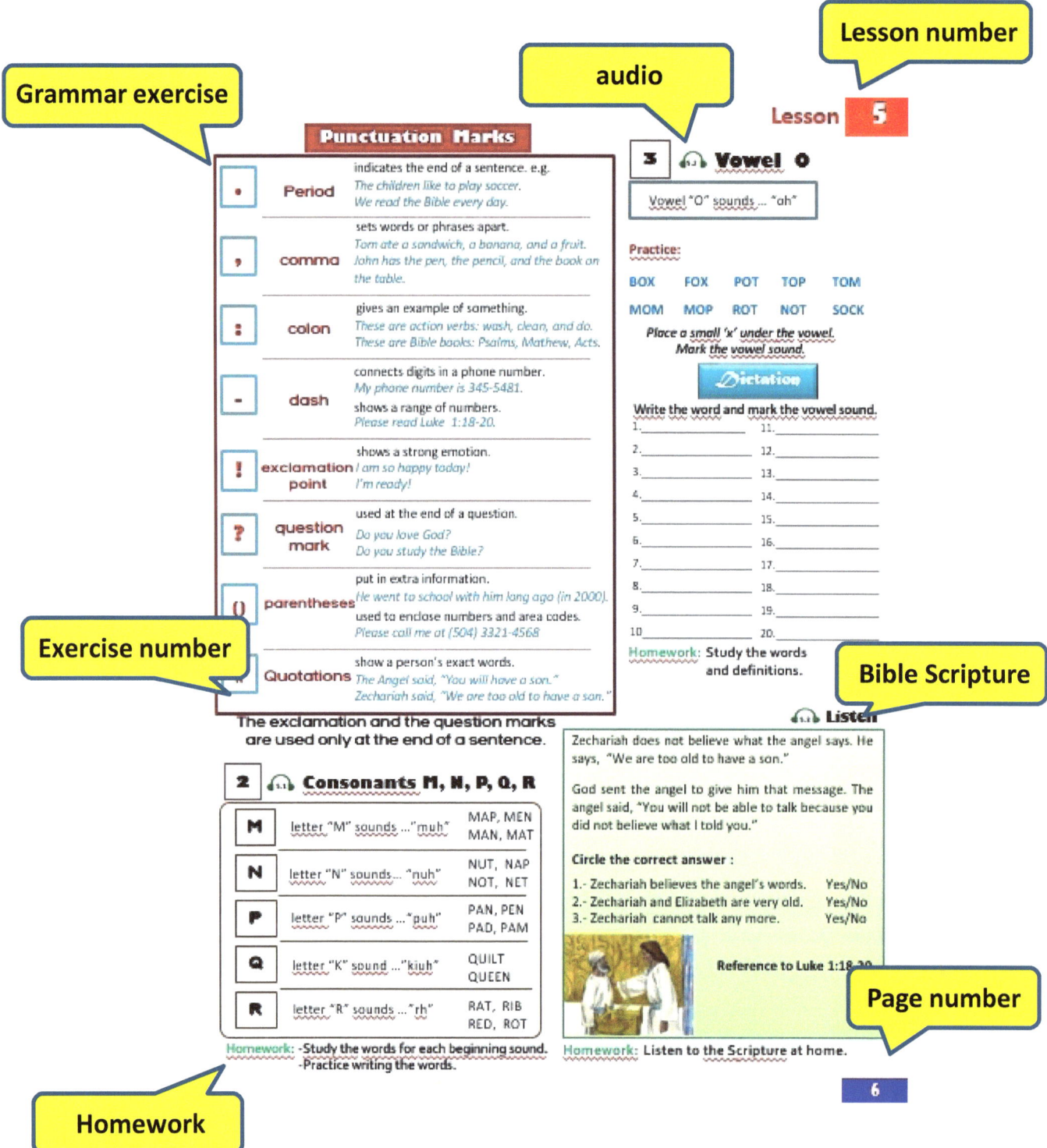

This page shows the way the lessons are organized in the book. Please explain this to students before starting to use the book.

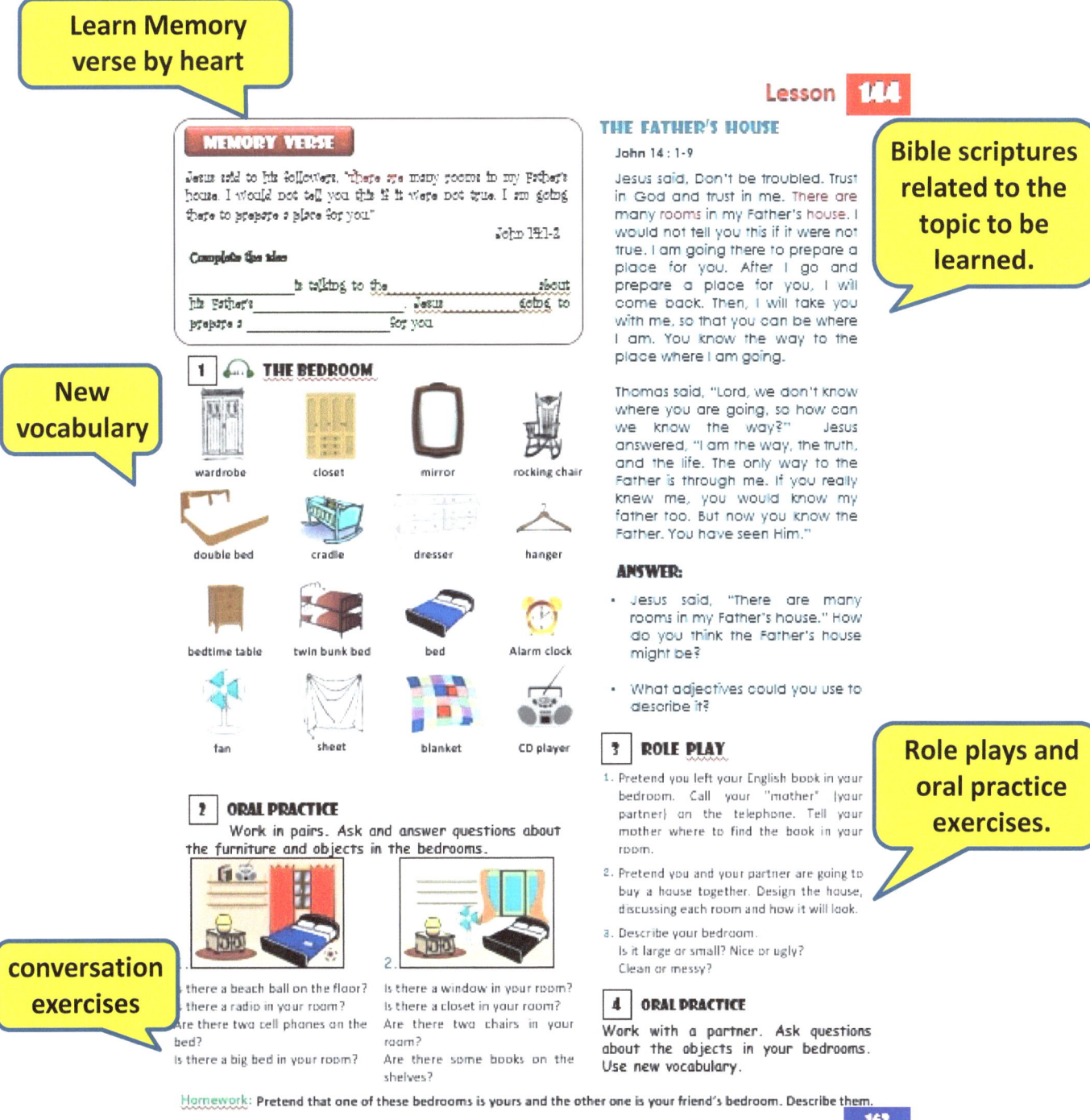

We aim to have conversational classes based in Bible topics and Bible Scriptures and stories to discuss in class.

New vocabulary words are introduced in each topic. Later on, students work in different oral practice exercises in which they use the new vocabulary words and are able to develop communicative skills.

Contents

Unit	Lessons	Description	Page
1		**UNIT I - INTRODUCTION AND OBJECTIVES**	1
	1-2	**INTRODUCTION TO PHONETICS** The alphabet Vowel 'a' Consonants b, d, f	2-3
	3-4	Consonants g, h, j, l Common words list 1 Take notes Vowel 'e'	4-5
	5-6	Punctuation marks Consonants m, n, p, q, r Vowel 'o'	6-7
	7-8	Common words list 2 Consonants s, t, v, w Vowel 'u'	8-9
	9-10	Common words list 3 Consonants s, y, z Vowel i Reading practice	10-11
	11-12	blends I : L- Blends R-blends Reading practice	12-13
	13-15	Blends II : S-blends 1 S-Blends 2 Reading	14-16
	16-17	Blend dictation Common words list 4 Bible characters	17-18

Contents

Unit	Lessons	Description	Page
2		UNIT II - INTRODUCTION AND OBJECTIVES	19
	18-19	Consonant digraphs More Consonant Digraphs Reading Practice Common Words list 5	20-21
	20-23	Double Letter Endings Special Ending Sounds More Special Ending Sounds Common Words List 6	22-24
	24-25	R – controlled vowels: One or Two Consonants Special Sounds	25-26
	26-27	Contractions Common Words List 7	27-28
	28-29	Long Vowel Sounds : 1. An Only Vowel 2. The Silent 'e' Skill: Long a Long i	29-30
3		UNIT III - INTRODUCTION AND OBJECTIVES	31
	30-31	Long 'o' Sound Long 'u' Sound Common Words List 8 Long 'e' Sound	32-35
	32-33	Rules for the Use of 'ke', 'k', 'sk', 'c' Reading Practice	36-37
	34-36	Soft 'C' sound Reading Practice Hard 'C' sound Reading Practice	38-40

Contents

Unit	Lessons	Description	Page
4		UNIT IV - INTRODUCTION AND OBJECTIVES	41
	37-39	Soft 'G' Sound Reading Practice Hard 'G' Sound	42-44
	40-41	3 Consonant Digraph I 3 Consonant Digraph II	45-46
	42-43	3 Consonant Digraph III Reading Practice 'dge' Ending Common Words list 9	47-48
	44-45	Adjacent Vowels I Reading Practice	49-50
	46-47	More Adjacent Vowels Reading Practice	51-52
	48-50	Words With OU/OW Reading Practice Words With AU/AW Common Words List 10	53-55
5		UNIT V - INTRODUCTION AND OBJECTIVES	56
	51-53	Words With 'OI/OY' Reading Practice	57-59

	54-55	Letter 'Y'
		  1. 'Y' as a consonant
		  2. 'Y' as a vowel
		  3. 'Y' with 'ai' sound
		  4. 'Y' as in 'Crypt'
			60-61

	56-57	More Words With 'Y'
		  1. 'Y' in silent 'e' skill
		  2. a vowel + 'Y'
		  3. 'Y' in a two syllable word
			62-63

	58-59	Two Syllable Words I Reading Practice	64-65
	60-61	Two Syllable Words II Bible Books - New Testament	66-67
	62-63	Two Syllable Words III	68-69

Contents

Unit	Lessons	Description	Page
6		**UNIT VI - INTRODUCTION AND OBJECTIVES**	70
	64-65	Prefixes	71-72
	66-67	Suffixes and Root Words	73-74
	68-69	Word Endings Multi-Syllable Words	75-76
	70-71	Special Vowel Combinations Special Vowel Sounds	77-78
7		**UNIT VII - INTRODUCTION AND OBJECTIVES**	79
	72-73	Who is God? Greeting and farewells Meeting people Common phrases	80-81
	74-75	Reading practice Dialogue Personal Information Verb to be	82-83
	76-77	Who is Jesus? Numbers from 0-1000 Jesus Feeds 5000 people	84-85
	78-79	Subject Pronouns Titles in English Possessive Adjectives Introduction: His, Her Interviews **Let's Talk About... Our Classmates**	86-87
		Unit 7 Summary	88

Contents

Units	Lessons	Description	Page
8		UNIT VIII - INTRODUCTION AND OBJECTIVES	89
	80-81	Countries and Nationalities	90-91
	82-83	Where are you from? Possessive adjectives II	92-93
	84	Let's Talk About... Building a Tower Landmarks Around The World	94
	85-87	Why to study the Bible? Classroom objects Demonstrative adjectives Let's Talk About...The classroom Our ESL Program	95-97
	88-89	Possessive Adjectives Commands	98-99
	90-92	Classroom Language Questions with Who Possessive Adjectives – People's Relationships Let's Talk About...Jesus Meets a Woman in Samaria	100-102
	92	Unit 8 Summary	103
9		UNIT IX - INTRODUCTION AND OBJECTIVES	104
	93	Why is it important to pray? The shapes The colors	105
	94-95	Opposite Adjectives I	106-107
	96-99	Opposite Adjectives II Let's Talk About... Daniel and His Friends	108-111
	100-103	Prepositions of Place I Prepositions of Place II Where are the objects?	112-115
	104-108	Singular and Plural Nouns Prepositions of place review Let's Talk About... The creation of the world Ordinal Numbers 1st to 20th	116-120
		Unit 9 - Summary	121

Contents

Units	Lessons	Description	Page
10		**UNIT X - INTRODUCTION AND OBJECTIVES**	**122**
	109-110	Feelings and Emotions Verb To Be	123-124
	111-112	The Family To Be - Contractions	125-126
	113	Let's Talk About…The Family	127
	114-115	Jobs and Occupations I To Be - Negative and Interrogative	128-129
	116-117	Jobs and Occupations II To Be - Review Short answers	130-131
	118	Let's Talk About… Jobs and Occupations Tips For a Successful Job Interview	132
		Unit 10 - Summary	133

Contents

Units	Lessons	Description	Page
11		UNIT XI - INTRODUCTION AND OBJECTIVES	134
	119-120	The Present Continuous Tense – Affirmative form Verbs I Every day activities What are you doing?	135-136
	121-122	The Present Continuous Tense – Negative / interrogative forms Verbs II	137-138
	123-124	The Past Continuous Tense – Affirmative form Verbs III Past Tense Expressions	139-140
	125	Let's Talk About… Family pictures The Big Catch	141
	126-127	The Weather	142-143
	128	Let's Talk About… Severe Weather Conditions Jesus Calms the Water	144
	129-130	The Simple Present Tense – Affirmative Form The Days of the Week	145-146
	131-132	The Simple Present Tense –Short answers Daily Routines I The Seasons of the Year Frequency Expressions	147-148
	133-134	The Months of The Year Daily Routines II The Simple Present Tense –Negative and Interrogative Forms Recess Activities Conjunctions	149-150
	135	Let's Talk About… Holidays and Celebrations	151
		Unit 11 – Summary	152

Contents

Units	Lessons	Description	Page
12		UNIT XII - INTRODUCTION AND OBJECTIVES	153
	136-137	The Simple Present Tense – Third Person Recess Activities II	154-155
	138-139	Adverbs of Frequency Action Verbs List IV	156-157
	140-141	Places to live – Where do you live? Parts of the House Verb There to Be – There is	158-159
	142-143	Verb There to Be – There are The Living room The Wise Man	160-161
	144-145	The bedroom Verb There to Be – Interrogative Form The Father's House	162-163
	146-147	The kitchen Verb to have – Present Short answers	164-165
	148-149	The bathroom Verb to have – Negative and Interrogative forms Verb to have – Third Person	166-167
	150-151	Verb to have – Past Tense Short Answers	168-169
	152	Let's Talk About… Places to live	170
		Unit 12 - Summary	171

UNIT 1

INTRODUCTION

In this unit, you will learn the names and sounds of the alphabet, as well as words beginning with each letter sound. You will learn a series of common words lists that will help you increase your vocabulary.

You will take dictations of words and be able to write sentences using the correct punctuation marks. You will practice reading and writing blends and identify words that have blends in them.

You will also learn about the life of Jesus Christ and the Bible books of the old testament.

OBJECTIVES

- Identify the letters and sounds of the alphabet.
- Read words with short vowel sounds and consonant sounds.
- Write words with each vowel and consonant.
- Use punctuation marks properly.
- Use common words from the lists to complete and to write sentences.
- Practice reading sentences and Bible scriptures.
- Write sentences.

Lesson 1

Introduction to Phonetics

1 🎧 1.1 **The Alphabet**

A B C D E
F G H I J
K L M N O
P Q R S T
U V W X Y Z

These are the "names" of the letters.
There are 26 letters in the English alphabet.

2 What letter is this?
Circle the letters you hear.

A B E G H J
K M P R T U
C V D O W Z

Zechariah and Elizabeth 🎧 1.2

They are Zechariah and Elizabeth. They are good people. They love God.

They are sad because they have no children. Elizabeth can not have a baby. She is very old.

Zechariah is in the Temple of the Lord and an angel of the Lord comes to him.

Reference to Luke 1 : 5-11

3 🎧 1.3 **Vowel A**

Vowel "A" sounds …'ah'

Read the words. Mark the symbol over the vowel.

| CAT | BAT | MAT | MAD | DAD | FAT | RAT |
| BAR | SAT | BAD | CAP | BAG | TAP | MAP |

The following words have a very similar sound:

CAN SAD PAN PAM FAN MAN RAN

4 🎧 1.4 **Consonants B, D, F**
Practice reading the words.

B	letter "B" sound… "buh"	BAG, BAT BAD
D	letter "D" sounds…"duh"	DAD, DAN
F	letter "F" sounds …"fuh"	FAN, FAR FACT

These words have "short vowel" sounds.

ă ĕ ĭ ŏ ŭ

5 Complete

1.-_____ are Zechariah and Elizabeth.

2.- They_____ good _____.
3.- They are_____ because Elizabeth can _____ have a _____. She _____ very old.
4.- Zechariah _____ in the_____.
An_____comes to him.

Homework: Listen to sounds of letters and words.
Practice writing the words.

Lesson 2

6 Spelling names
Answer, then practice spelling the names.

1.- What is your first name?
_____

2.- What is your teacher's name?
_____

3.- Write the names of four friends. Spell each.
_____   _____
_____   _____

7 Dictation

1.-_____   6.-_____
2.-_____   7.-_____
3.-_____   8.-_____
4.-_____   9.-_____
5.-_____   10_____

At Home

1 Answer
Circle the correct answer.

1.-Every word has at least one:
a) period   b) capital letter   c) vowel

2.- The letters 'a, e, i' are examples of :
a) consonants   b) short sound   c) vowels

3.- There are ___ letters in the English alphabet.
a) 27   b) 26   c) 20

2 Write the name of each letter.

A   C   E   G
___ ___ ___ ___

H   I   K   M
___ ___ ___ ___

N   P   Q   T
___ ___ ___ ___

U   W   Y   Z
___ ___ ___ ___

3 Write the words that start with each beginning sound:

B _____
  _____

D _____
  _____

F _____
  _____

4 Write the words that have the 'a' sound.

1.-_____   10.-_____
2.-_____   11.-_____
3.-_____   12.-_____
4.-_____   13.-_____
5.-_____   14.-_____
6.-_____   15.-_____
7.-_____   16.-_____
8.-_____   17.-_____
9.-_____   18.-_____

5 Label the picture with the words from above.

Lesson 3

1 🎧 3.1 Consonats G, H, J, L

Practice pronouncing the letter sounds and the words.

G	letter "G" sounds ... "guh"	GO, GET BEG, GAS
H	letter "H" sounds ... "huh"	HAT, HEN HAM, HOT
J	letter "J" sounds ... "juh"	JET, JACK JAM, JIM
L	letter "L" sounds ... "luh"	LAP, LAMP LET, LEG

2 🎧 3.2 Common Words List 1

Underline the common words you find in the sentences.

I	a	the	to	no	it	is	you
	and	at	in	my	not		

1. I am a student.
2. It is my bag!
3. It is my red pen!
4. Dad is at the lab.
5. Is the bag in the car?
6. You are Sam.
7. Dad has a car.
8. It is his pet, Rex.
9. I am not a boy.
10. The bat is small.
11. The hen is big.
12. I am not a bad boy.
13. This is not my cap.
14. My car is not big.
15. The pig is in the pen.
16. Is the car blue?
17. The hen has ten eggs.
18. The man is on the jet.
19. The woman is my mom.
20. Are you Ted?

Homework: Practice reading and writing words and sentences.

The visit of the angel 🎧 3.3
Reference to Luke 1:12-17

Zechariah is afraid to see the angel. The angel says: "God heard your prayer. Your wife Elizabeth will have a son, and his name will be John." He will be a great man for the Lord.

Complete:

1.- Zechariah is afraid of the _____.
2.- The angel says, "_____ heard your _____. Your _____ Elizabeth will have a _____, and his name will be _____.
3.- He will be a _____ man for the _____."

3 Take Notes

> Upper case letters are used to write proper names.

> Upper case letters start a sentence.

> A phrase is a part of a sentence. It gives an incomplete idea.

> A sentence is a group of words that give a complete idea or thought.

Homework: Write 3 examples of sentences and phrases.

4 🎧 3.4 Vowel E

> vowel "E" sounds 'i'

Have students place the symbol for short sound over the vowel.

BED	TED	NET	SET	LENT
MET	PET	MEN	HEN	MESS
BEN	SENT	BET	SEND	

Homework: Practice reading and writing the words.

Upper case letters:

Lower case letters:

| a | b | t | c |

Homework:

Practice reading and writing new words.

At Home

Lesson 4

1. Circle the sentences. Underline the phrases.

1.- My name is Juan.
2.- I am a disciple.
3.- I am not
4.- I live in
5.- It is big.
6.- He is tall.
7.- That car is red.
8.- is good

2. Write words that have the 'e' sound.

1._____
2._____
3._____
4._____
5._____
6._____
7._____
8._____
9._____
10._____
11._____
12._____
13._____

4. Write words with each sound.

G	H	J	L

5. Circle the correct answer.

1.- These are examples of upper case letters :
a) A,B,C   b) a,b,c   c) a,e,i,o,u

2.- These letters are used to start a sentence :
a) lower case   b) upper case   c) vowels

3.- Upper case letters are also used to write ____.
a) common nouns   b) proper names   c) names of things

4.- A sentence gives a complete ___.
a) sound   b) idea   c) vowel sound

5.- A __ is a part of a sentence. It gives an incomplete idea:
a) question   b) phrase   c) period

6.- Are specific names of people, places, or animals:
a) common names   b) vowels   c) proper names

6. Circle the upper case letters.

a   B   e   G   H   i   K   M   P
q   R   T   s   U   V   x   y   n

3. Label the pictures.

Lesson 5

Punctuation Marks

.	Period	indicates the end of a sentence. e.g. *The children like to play soccer. We read the Bible every day.*
,	comma	sets words or phrases apart. *Tom ate a sandwich, a banana, and a fruit. John has the pen, the pencil, and the book on the table.*
:	colon	gives an example of something. *These are action verbs: wash, clean, and do. These are Bible books: Psalms, Mathew, Acts.*
-	dash	connects digits in a phone number. *My phone number is 345-5481.* shows a range of numbers. *Please read Luke 1:18-20.*
!	exclamation point	shows a strong emotion. *I am so happy today! I'm ready!*
?	question mark	used at the end of a question. *Do you love God? Do you study the Bible?*
( )	parentheses	put in extra information. *He went to school with him long ago (in 2000).* used to enclose numbers and area codes. *Please call me at (504) 3321-4568*
" "	Quotations	show a person's exact words. *The Angel said, "You will have a son." Zechariah said, "We are too old to have a son."*

The exclamation and the question marks are used only at the end of a sentence.

2 5.1 Consonants M, N, P, Q, R

M	letter "M" sounds ..."muh"	MAP, MEN MAN, MAT
N	letter "N" sounds... "nuh"	NUT, NAP NOT, NET
P	letter "P" sounds ..."puh"	PAN, PEN PAD, PAM
Q	letter "K" sound ..."kiuh"	QUILT QUEEN
R	letter "R" sounds ..."rh"	RAT, RIB RED, ROT

Homework: -Study the words for each beginning sound.
-Practice writing the words.

3 5.2 Vowel O

Vowel "O" sounds ... "oh"

Practice:

BOX   FOX   POT   TOP   TOM
MOM   MOP   ROT   NOT   SOCK

Place a small 'x' under the vowel.
Mark the vowel sound.

Dictation

Write the word and mark the vowel sound.

1._____ 11._____
2._____ 12._____
3._____ 13._____
4._____ 14._____
5._____ 15._____
6._____ 16._____
7._____ 17._____
8._____ 18._____
9._____ 19._____
10._____ 20._____

Homework: Study the words and definitions.

5.3 Listen

Zechariah does not believe what the angel says. He says, "We are too old to have a son."

God sent the angel to give him that message. The angel said, "You will not be able to talk because you did not believe what I told you."

Circle the correct answer :

1.- Zechariah believes the angel's words.   Yes/No
2.- Zechariah and Elizabeth are very old.   Yes/No
3.- Zechariah cannot talk any more.   Yes/No

Reference to Luke 1:18-20

Homework: Listen to the Scripture at home.

Lesson 6

At Home

1 Name each punctuation mark. Write the missing punctuation marks.

. _____   Carlos likes to play soccer every day _____

, _____   I love to eat apples ___ bananas ___ and grapes. _____

: _____   These are examples of nouns ___ people, dog, and pen. _____

- _____   I love the scripture in Isaiah 43: 2 ___ 4. _____

! _____   I am so tired today _____

? _____   Is this your new English book _____

( ) _____   My phone number is ___ 605 ___ 8743-9023. _____

" " _____   Mary replied to the angel, ___ I am the Lord's servant. _____

Homework: Write two examples of each punctuation in your notebook.

2 Write the words you learned with each beginning sound.

M	N	P	R
___	___	___	___
___	___	___	___
___	___	___	___

Homework: Practice reading and writing the words. Learn the meanings of the words.

4 Complete the Scripture.

Zechariah does_____believe what the _____ says. He says, "We_____too old to have a _____."

_____sends the_____to give him that_____. The angel said to him "You will not be able to talk because you did not_____what I told you."

- Who could not talk?
- What is the angel's name?

3 Write the words that have the "O" sound.

1.-_____   6.-_____
2.-_____   7.-_____
3.-_____   8.-_____
4.-_____   9.-_____
5.-_____   10._____

Homework: Practice reading and writing the words. Learn the meanings of the words.

5 Label the pictures.

Lesson 7

1 🎧 7.1 Common Words List 2

Underline the common words you find in the sentences.

on	are	what	hat	that	do	has
he	me	they	your	this	be	his

1. The cat is on the bed.
2. Is this pen for me?
3. They are my Mom and Dad.
4. Efrain has a red hat.
5. I have a blue hat.
6. Is that your new car?
7. This is what I need.
8. Is this his old bat?
9. Is that your pen?
10. I have his pen.
11. Are they in this class?
12. Is this your cap?
13. He has a big bat.
14. Are they your friends?
15. The man has a hat in his hand.
16. Your dad has to be here today.
17. Those are not his toys.
18. Do you have friends?
19. They are on the mat.

Homework: Study common words.
Practice reading and writing sentences.

Final Sound ng

STRO<u>ng</u>   SO<u>ng</u>

Each letter keeps its sound 'ng'.

2 🎧 7.2 Consonants S, T, V, W

Practice pronouncing the letter sounds and the words.

S	letter "S" sounds …"suh'	SAT, SIT, SET, SAM
T	letter "T" sounds …"tuh"	TAP, TIP TED, TOP
V	letter "V" sounds …"vh"	VAN, VET, VANISH
W	letter "W" sounds …"uoh"	WEB, WET, WIN, WON

Homework: -Study the sounds of letters and words.
-Practice writing the words.

3 🎧 7.3 Vowel U

Vowel "U" sounds … "uh"

Practice:

UP	UNDER	MUG	UGLY	NUT
US	UNCLE	TUB	SUN	CUT
CUP	UMBRELLA	SUM	LUCK	PUTT

This sound is not the same as "u" in Spanish.

Write the word and mark the vowel sounds.

1._____   9._____
2._____   10_____
3._____   11_____
4._____   12_____
5._____   13_____
6._____   14_____
7._____   15_____
8._____   16_____

Homework: Practice writing the words.
Learn definitions of words.

🎧 7.4 Listen

Zechariah comes out of the Temple but he can not speak. So the people know that he saw a vision inside the Temple. Later, Elizabeth becomes pregnant.

Reference to Luke 1:21-25

Answer:

1. What happens to Zechariah?

2. Where did Zechariah see a vision?

3. What happens to Elizabeth?

Homework: Listen to the scripture at home.

Lesson 8

At Home

1 Write the sentence from lesson 7 exercise 1 that describes each picture.

_____

_____

_____

_____

_____

2 Write the words that have each sound.

| S | T | V | W |

____ ____ ____ ____
____ ____ ____ ____
____ ____ ____ ____

3 Label the pictures.

_____   _____

   3+1=4
_____   _____

_____   _____

_____   _____

_____   _____

🎧 8.1 **Paraphrased from Luke 1:56-64**

Elizabeth had a boy. The Lord was very good to her. They named the boy John as the angel said. Everyone was surprised. Then Zechariah could talk again, and he praised God.

Answer:

1) What was the baby's name?

2) What did Zechariah do when he talked again?

3) Who was surprised?

Every sentence begins with a capital letter.

Lesson 9

1 🎧 9.1 COMMON WORDS LIST 3

day	work	was	for	mother
of	from	she	boy	father
man	here	red	house	friends
some	there	have	today	

1. My father has to work all day.
2. The cat was not on the red rug.
3. I go to work every day.
4. This is from Kevin. It is for you.
5. We were looking for you.
6. Is your mother at your house?
7. I was not at work yesterday.
8. Gerardo, are some of your friends here?
9. The man has a big house.
10. Some students are at your house.
11. The boy has a good mother.
12. She was at home today.
13. We were not at work today.
14. My friends are from Santa Barbara.
15. Yes, they are not from here.
16. I have to work all day today.
17. Is the big bag here?

Homework: Practice reading and writing words and sentences.

🎧 9.4 Listen

Reference to Luke 1:26-33

God sends the angel Gabriel to a virgin girl who lives in Nazareth. She will marry a man named Joseph. Her name is Mary.

The angel says to her, "You will have a baby boy. His name will be Jesus. He will be great. People will call him the Son of God."

Answer

1. What does the angel tell Mary?

2. How does Mary feel?

Homework: Listen to the Scripture at home.

2 🎧 9.2 Consonants X, Y, Z

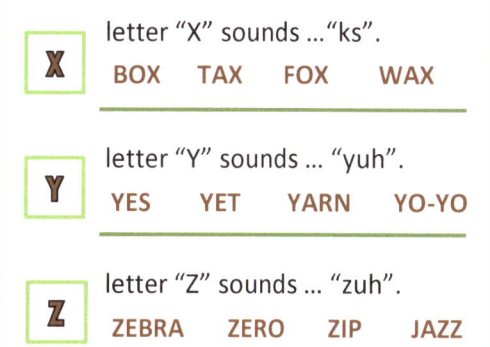

X	letter "X" sounds …"ks".
	BOX TAX FOX WAX

Y	letter "Y" sounds … "yuh".
	YES YET YARN YO-YO

Z	letter "Z" sounds … "zuh".
	ZEBRA ZERO ZIP JAZZ

Homework: Learn definitions of words.

3 🎧 9.3 Vowel i

Vowel "I" sounds … "ai"

Practice:

PIG	SIT	HIT	INK	BIT	PIN
TIM	FIN	SIN	SID	BIB	RING
FIX	LID	RIB	FIT	BIN	WIND

4 Reading Practice

1. Celso has a red hat.
2. My bed is not so big.
3. My father is here today.
4. Ted has to work all day today.
5. Father said to go home.
6. The hen has ten eggs.
7. This is my new car.
8. The pigs are in big.
9. The dogs are in the house.
10. This is my pet cat.
11. I had a blue cap.
12. What are you doing mom?
13. My father is in his new car.

Homework: Practice reading the sentences.

10

Lesson 10

At Home

1 Complete the sentences with the words in the box.

| work | mother | from | boy | father | day |
| house | friends | here | man | | red |

1. I go to my mother's house every _____.
2. My father likes to _____ hard.
4. I have many _____ at church.
5. My _____ lives _____.
6. My _____ is a good man.
7. The _____ lost his_____toy car.
8. She lives in an old _____ .
9. My uncle comes _____ the United States.
10. I do not know that_____.

2 Crossword

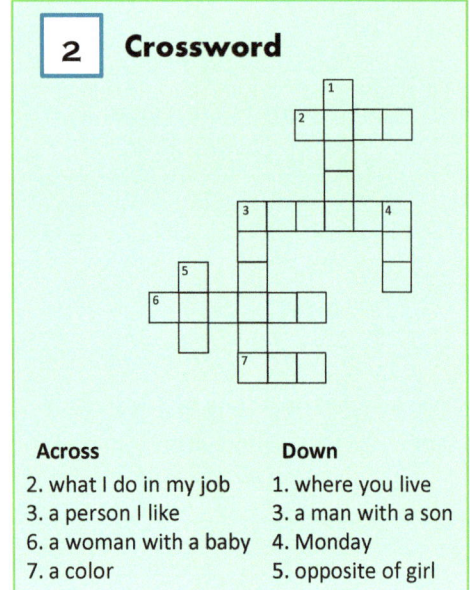

Across
2. what I do in my job
3. a person I like
6. a woman with a baby
7. a color

Down
1. where you live
3. a man with a son
4. Monday
5. opposite of girl

3 Write the words with each letter.

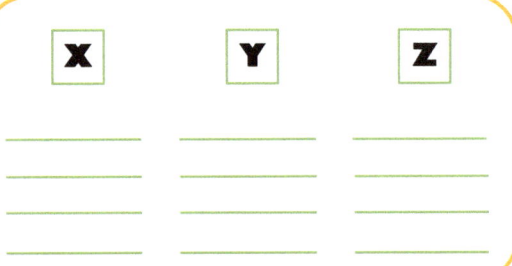

4 Circle the words that have the short 'i' sound.

fin	Tim	box	lung	sit
pin	can	ring	time	lime
bin	bib	pig	send	rat

5 Write the missing letter to form the words.

1. wo__k   5. r__d   9. fr__m   9. y__rn
2. her__   6. bo__   10. th__re   10. t__x
3. m__n   7. fis__   11. zebr__   11. hav__
4. s__m__   8. da__   12. zer__   12. toda__

6 Label the pictures.

Lesson 11

Blends I

BLENDS ARE 2 OR 3 CONSONANTS, STANDING TOGETHER. EACH LETTER KEEPS ITS OWN SOUND.

L Blends: bl, cl, fl, gl, pl, sl

R Blends: br, cr, dr, fr, gr, pr, tr

bl
blend
bless
black
blue
block

cl
clap
clam
clip
class
clock

fl
flow
fly
flag
flat
float

br
brick
bread
brown
break
Brad

cr
crib
crop
crab
cross
crack

fr
fry
Fred
frog
frost
fraud

gl
glue
glow
glad

pl
plum
plane
please
play

sl
slow
sled
slim
sleep
slide

gr
grass
green
grow
grape

pr
press
price
prince
prize

tr
trap
troop
treat
train

dr   drum   dress   drop

Homework:
Practice reading and writing words with blends.

2 Reading

Underline the blends you find in the sentences.

1. She has black hair.
2. I pray God every day.
3. I try to do my best in class.
4. The boy got a prize today.
5. The children play soccer.
6. My friend did not like the dress.
7. He wants to play the drums.
8. Frogs and toads are green.
9. The grass is tall.
10. The flag pole is brown.
11. Give me some grapes please.

Homework: Practice reading and writing sentences.

3 Writing

Write the blend needed to complete the words.

_____ost   _____ick   _____um
_____ass   _____ap   _____ane
_____ad   _____ize   _____ain
_____ead   _____y   _____end
_____ow   _____ock   _____ease
_____ed   _____oat   _____ow
_____ag   _____ow   _____aud
_____ip   _____op   _____ab
_____um   _____ess   _____ice
_____ape   _____een   _____ay
_____im   _____ince   _____ue

12

At Home

Lesson 12

L Blends: bl, cl, fl, gl, pl, sl

1 Label the pictures.

2 Write the missing word to complete each sentence.

1. The turtle is _____.
2. The _____ is brown.
3. The _____ is blue.
4. The _____ is purple

5. The boy likes to_____.
6. The _____ is red and green.
7. The _____ is black.
8. The _____ is red.

R Blends: br, cr, dr, fr, gr, pr, tr

3 Label the pictures.

4 Write the missing word to complete each sentence.

1. The _____ is green and yellow.
2. The _____ is brown.
3. The _____ is black.
4. The _____ is green.

5. The _____ is fresh.
6. The _____ is blue.
7. The house has a_____.
8. The _____ are purple.

Lesson 13

Blends II

 S Blends: 8 have 2 letters
sc, sk, sl, sm, sn, sp, st, sw

5 S – Blends have 3 letters
scr, spr, str, spl, squ

sc	sk	sp
Scott	skull	spoil
scan	skill	spam
score	sketch	spell

sm	sw	st
small	sweet	stop
smell	sweat	stem
Smith	swan	stamp
		store

sn			
	snail	snore	snow
	snack	snake	sneeze

scr	spr	str
scrub	spray	street
script	Sprite	strike
screen	spring	stripe

spl	squ
split	square
splash	squirrel
splendid	

2 READING PRACTICE

Underline the blends you find in the sentences.

1. Scott likes to drink Sprite.
2. Please give me the stamp.
3. Could you please buy some fruit?
4. I like the flowers in spring.
5. There is a squirrel on that tree!
6. The boy did not spell one word.
7. She has a big swan.
8. The screen of my tv. is big.
9. I am afraid of snakes.
10. That is Main street.

Books of The Bible

OLD TESTAMENT
- Genesis
- Exodus
- Leviticus
- Numbers
- Deuteronomy

Answer:

1. Which of these books have you read?

3. Are you reading any of these books now?

4. What is the first book of the Bible?

3 WRITING

Write the blend needed to complete the words.

____an	____ore	____ore	____oil
____all	____endid	____ull	____ail
____ill	____am	____eat	____ore
____it	____eet	____ike	____amp
____ell	____ub	____ipt	____ing
____em	____op	____irrel	____ash
____etch	____ay	____eet	____ap
____ell	____ipe	____ake	____een

Homework: Practice reading and writing words with blends.

GENESIS: Describes the creation.

EXODUS: Relates the events of the departure of Israel from Egypt.

LEVITICUS: The law of God given as rules to the Hebrew people.

NUMBERS: The story of the Israelites through the desert.

DEUTERONOMY: Relates the Ten Commandments and other laws given in to the people.

Homework: Study the list of Bible books.

Lesson 14

At Home

S Blends have 2 letters: sc, sk, sl, sm, sn, sp, st, sw

1 Label the pictures.

_____ _____ _____ _____ _____ _____

_____ _____ _____ _____ _____ _____

2 Write the missing word to complete each sentence.

1. The _____ sign is red.
2. The _____ is green.
3. The _____ is slow.
4. I need a _____ for the envelop.
5. The girl likes to _____ the flowers.
6. The cupcake is _____.
7. My father and I _____ very loud.
8. I can _____ the word 'welcome'.

S – Blends have 3 letters: scr, spr, str, spl, squ

3 Label the pictures.

_____ _____ _____ _____ _____

_____ _____ _____ _____ _____

4 Write the missing word to complete each sentence.

1. Zebras have many _____.
2. Do not cross the _____ by yourself.
3. The square is _____.
4. There are many flowers in _____.
5. The _____ eats nuts.
6. I like to _____ the water.
7. Martha has a new hair _____.
8. The computer has a wide _____.

Lesson 16

1 BLEND DICTATION
Write the word you hear.
Circle the blend in each word.

1. _____   11. _____
2. _____   12. _____
3. _____   13. _____
4. _____   14. _____
5. _____   15. _____
6. _____   16. _____
7. _____   17. _____
8. _____   18. _____
9. _____   19. _____
10. _____   20. _____

2 16.1 COMMON WORDS LIST 4
Read the words and sentences.
Underline the words from the list you find.

their	other	had	us	said	does
will	who	give	as	word	when
once	were	how	or	use	many

1. They want to use their new car.
2. Our children live with us.
3. Will you give them their gift?
4. I have their pen.
5. Can you go with us?
6. They said they were friends.
7. I do not use this word.
8. Their friends were here.
9. They had a small car before.
10. Who will use the tablet first?
11. How do you feel?
12. I had a big truck once.
13. How do I say this word in English?
14. Will you come with us?

Practice reading and writing words with blends.

3 Complete
Use the words in the box to complete the description of each book.

GENESIS
Describes the _____ of the world.

EXODUS
Relates the event of the departure of _____ from _____.

LEVITICUS
The _____ of God given as rules to the _____ people.

NUMBERS
The story of the _____ through the _____.

DEUTERONOMY
Relates the _____ Commandments and other laws given before.

EGYPT
LAW
CREATION
ISRAELITES
ISRAEL
DESERT
TEN
HEBREW

Bible Characters

Adam: The first man on Earth.
Eve: The first woman.
Moses: The man used by God to free Israel from slavery.
Pharaoh: The ruler of the old Egypt.

4 Write any other words you know with each blend.

sc	sp	sm	str	sm	st	spr
___	___	___	___	___	___	___
___	___	___	___	___	___	___
___	___	___	___	___	___	___

Lesson 17

At Home

Reference to Luke 1:34-38

Mary said to the angel, "How can this happen? I am still a virgin." The angel said to Mary, "The Holy Spirit will come to you, and the power of the Most High God will cover you. The baby will be holy and will be called the Son of God. Elizabeth is pregnant. She is very old, but she is going to have a son. God can do anything!"

Answer:
1.- What was the woman's name?
2.- Who came to see her?
3.- What was going to happen to her?
4.- What was special about this baby?

2 Writing
Write the words in order to form sentences related to the Scripture in Luke 1:34-38.

1. The angel / Mary / visits
   _____

2. pregnant / is / Elizabeth
   _____

3. Mary / afraid / is
   _____

4. is / a good / woman
   _____

3 Old Testament

Joshua	I Samuel	I Chronicles
Judges	II Samuel	II Chronicles
Ruth	I and II Kings	Ezra

JOSHUA
The story of the conquest of Canaan.

JUDGES
The history of the nation from Joshua to Samson.

RUTH
The story of the ancestors of the royal family of Judah.

I SAMUEL
The story of the nation during the time of Samuel and the reign of Saul.

II SAMUEL
Story of the reign of David.

I AND II KINGS
Relate part of the history of Israel. Narrates the reigns of Saul and David.

I AND II CHRONICLES
The histories of the kingdoms of Judah and Israel.

EZRA
The return of the Jews from the captivity of Babylon. The rebuilding of the temple.

Answer
Match the Bible character with its description. Write the letter of the word on the line provided.

_____ a great prophet of Israel.

_____ the second king of the kingdom of Israel.

_____ the first king of the kingdom of Israel.

_____ Moses' assistant who became the leader of the Israelite tribes after the death of Moses.

_____ one of the last judges of Israel who had supernatural strength given by God.

_____ a Moabitess who followed Naomi as she returned to Bethlehem.

| a) Samson | b) Samuel | c) Saul |
| d) David | e) Ruth | f) Joshua |

Homework: Study the Bible characters.

4 Writing
Write the words in order to form sentences.

1. The boy / tall / is
   _____

2. happy / I / am
   _____

3. a student / am / I
   _____

4. The apple / red / is
   _____

UNIT 2

INTRODUCTION

In this unit, you will learn more common words and some words with consonant digraphs, words with double letter endings and special sounds.

Later, you will practice adding 'ing' to verbs, and learn words with R-Controlled vowels. You will also practice how to write contractions.

Finally, you will learn some words with long vowel sounds and the rules to read them correctly.

OBJECTIVES

- Write words with each vowel and consonant.
- Learn words with double letter endings and special ending sounds.
- Learn more common words.
- Learn words with R-Controlled Vowels.
- Write and use contractions.
- Read sentences and Bible scriptures.
- Write sentences.

Lesson 18

1. CONSONANT DIGRAPHS 🎧 18.1

Consonant digraphs can start or end a word.

sh
- shoe   shot
- fish   wish
- shop   wash
- cash   ship
- shed   short

ch
- chick   teach
- chip   rich
- lunch   much
- chin   such
- chop   bench
- chest   match

Homework: Practice writing the words.
Learn definitions of words.

2. MORE CONSONANT DIGRAPHS 🎧 18.2

Read the words. Practice each sound.

PH	Sounds 'F' — PHILIPPIANS, PHOTOGRAPH
KN	Sounds 'N' — KNEE, KNEEL, KNOT, KNIFE
CK	Sounds 'K' — CHECK, BLOCK, SICK, BACK
GN	Sounds 'N' — GNAT, GNOME, GNARL
WR	Sounds 'R' — WRITE, WROTE, WRIST, WRAP

Homework: Practice writing the words.

3. READING PRACTICE 🎧 18.3

Circle the words that have 'ch' sound.
Underline the words with 'sh' sound.

1. I wish to buy a new pair of shoes.
2. Do I need cash for the fish?
3. Teach me how to pitch the ball.
4. I had chips and soda for lunch.
5. How much do I need?
6. He saw a t.v. show this morning.
7. Did they catch all the balls in the match?
8. Dad does not watch t.v. He prefers to wash his car.
9. I saw some chicks at the pet shop.
10. He sits on that bench for lunch every day.

Homework: Practice reading and writing the sentences.

4. COMMON WORDS LIST 5 🎧 18.4

Circle the common words found in the sentences.

men	blue	brother	each	them	like
color	nothing	her	before	make	help
home	ask	thing	why	full	tell

1. I have an older brother.
2. The men did nothing bad.
3. What color do you like?
4. Each of you has to ask for help.
5. Why did you call them?
6. I have nothing to tell them.
7. All the men are very happy.
8. Why did he ask for help?
9. Did you tell them what I did?
10. My brother is full of joy.
11. Do you like this color?

Homework: Practice writing words and sentences.

Dictation

1. _____
2. _____
3. _____
4. _____
5. _____
6. _____
7. _____
8. _____
9. _____
10. _____
11. _____
12. _____

OLD TESTAMENT

Nehemiah
Esther
Job
Psalms
Proverbs
Ecclesiastes
Song of Songs
Isaiah

Answer:
1.- Have you read these books?
2.- Which is your favorite book?

NEHEMIAH
An account of the rebuilding of the temple and the city.

ESTHER
The story of a Jewess who becomes queen of Persia.

JOB
The story and trials of a holy man.

PSALMS
A collection of poems to worship God.

PROVERBS
The wise sayings of Solomon.

ECCLESIASTES
A collection of poems respecting the vanity of earthly things.

SONG OF SONGS
Songs about married love and the human body as a creation of God.

ISAIAH
Prophecies about God and his people Israel.

At Home

Lesson 19

1 Label the pictures with words that have the sounds of 'sh' and 'ch'.

2 Write the words that have each sound.

PH	KN
CK	GN
WR	

3 Write words that contain each of the digraphs.

sh   **ch**

4 Complete the sentences with the words from the box.

| like | color | her | full | help | home | why | tell |

1. I need to go _____.
2. Green is a nice _____.
3. _____ are you angry?
4. This glass is _____ of water.
5. I _____ to eat pizza.
6. Can you _____ me please?
7. Can you _____ me your name?
8. I will visit _____ tomorrow.

Complete the statements with the words from the box.

NEHEMIAH
An account of the rebuilding of the _____ and the _____.

ESTHER
The story of a Jewess who becomes _____ of Persia.

JOB
The story and trials of a _____ _____ man.

PSALMS
A collection of _____ to worship _____.

PROVERBS
The _____ sayings of _____.

| TEMPLE |
| WISE |
| SOLOMON |
| QUEEN |
| CITY |
| GOD |
| JEWISH |
| HOLY |
| POEMS |
| EDOM |

Lesson 20

1 🎧 20.1 Double Letter Endings

Repeat the words. Circle the double letter ending in each word.

SS

CLASS	BRASS	MASS	PASS
LESS	DRESS	TESS	MESS
MISS	KISS	HISS	STRESS

FF

STAFF	PUFF	CUFF	CLIFF

ZZ

JAZZ	FIZZ		

LL

BALL	CALL	FALL	TALL
WALL	MALL	TELL	WELL
BELL	SMELL	JILL	SKILL
MILL	SPILL	KILL	STILL
BILL	DOLL	SKULL	GULL

Vowel 'A' with double 'L' has the sound of 'AW' as in saw.

If the small word ends in the sound of 'S, F, Z, L', double the consonant. Exceptions: is, as, his, has, was.

2 🎧 20.2 Special Ending Sounds

ang	*ing*	*ong*	*ung*
sang	sing	wrong	lung
hang	sting	song	
rang	ring	strong	
gang	bring		
	king		

🎧 20.4 More Ending Sounds

ank	*ink*	*onk*	*unk*
sank	sink	honk	junk
bank	stink		trunk
*ankle	pink		skunk
tank	wink		
blank	shrink		

*These letter combinations are also used at the beginning of the words as in 'ankle'

3 🎧 20.5 Common Words List 6

Underline the common words you find in the sentences.

see	name	him	just	form	great
end	say	also	play	small	same	come
put	sentence	too	where	now	need

1. What is your name?
2. Do you want to come with him?
3. Where can I put my book?
4. I need a new book.
5. This sentence ends with a period.
6. What do they say?
7. Do they want to play?
8. Where are you now?
9. Will you come tomorrow?
10. This game is great!
11. You just need one more sentence.
12. These two words mean the same.
13. Can you please say your name.
14. What does the sentence need at the end?
15. Come! Where are you going?

Homework: Practice writing words and sentences.

Sentences:
1.- We sang a new song at church yesterday.
2.- He learns about the lungs in his class.
3.- What is wrong in this math problem?
4.- The king has a golden ring.
5.- The alarm clock rang twice today.
6.- My friend is a strong man.
7.- Will they hang out tonight?
8.- A bee almost stings my leg.

Sentences:
1.- The stone sank to the bottom of the river.
2.- My brother has to go to the bank.
3.- The boy has a toy tank.
4.- I left the exercise in blank.
5.- I think my brother will come tomorrow.
6.- I do not like to eat junk food.
7.- I will put the bags in the trunk of the car.

🎧 20.6 Reference to Matthew 1:19-21

Mary's husband, Joseph, is a good man. He does not want to cause her public disgrace, so he plans to divorce her secretly, but an angel from the Lord came to him in a dream and told him not to be afraid to accept Mary as his wife because the baby inside her was from the Holy Spirit.

"She will give birth to a son named Jesus. Give him that name because he will save his people from their sins", He said.

Answer:

1.- What was the baby's name?
2.- Who came to Joseph in a dream?

Lesson 21

At Home

1 COMPLETE
Complete the sentences with the double letter ending words in the box.

| Miss. | class | kiss | pass | doll | mall | fall | call | dress | Bill |

1. I like my English _____.
2. The girl gave the baby a _____.
3. Please _____ me the salt.
4. _____ is a nice season.
5. The girl has a new _____.
6. She is _____ Gonzales, my English teacher.
7. Let's go to the _____.
8. I will go with Andrea and _____.
9. My mother has a new _____.
10. Sorry! I will _____ you later.

2 Label the pictures.

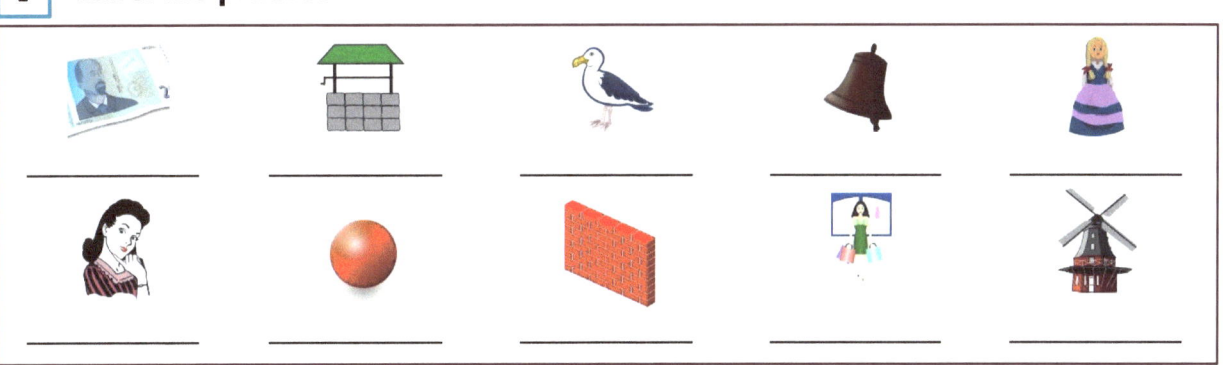

3 WRITING
Complete the sentences with the words in the box.

| pink | ankle | ring | sing | strong | song | trunk | bank | tank | king |

1. The boy has a toy _____.
2. The boxes are in the car's _____.
3. He is a _____ man.
4. They _____ very well.
5. I like to listen to that _____.
6. Strawberry ice-cream is color _____.
7. I hurt my _____ during the game.
8. The girl is wearing a golden _____.
9. I need to pay my bills at the _____.
10. The _____ lives in a big castle.

4 ANSWER

Reference to Matthew 1:19-21

Write T (True) or F (False.)

_____ 1. Mary's husband is called Joseph.
_____ 2. Joseph is not a good man.
_____ 3. The angel of the Lord came to Joseph in a dream.
_____ 4. The angel told him not to marry her.
_____ 5. The angel said the baby's name was John.
_____ 6. The angel said that the baby was from the Holy Spirit.

At Home

Special Letter Endings

Lesson 22

1 WRITE
Write the words you learned with each letter ending.

SS

1._____ 7._____
2._____ 8._____
3._____ 9._____
4._____ 10._____
5._____ 11._____
6._____ 12._____

LL

1._____ 7._____ 13._____
2._____ 8._____ 14._____
3._____ 9._____ 15._____
4._____ 10._____ 16._____
5._____ 11._____ 17._____
6._____ 12._____ 18._____

2 Label the pictures with words that have special endings.

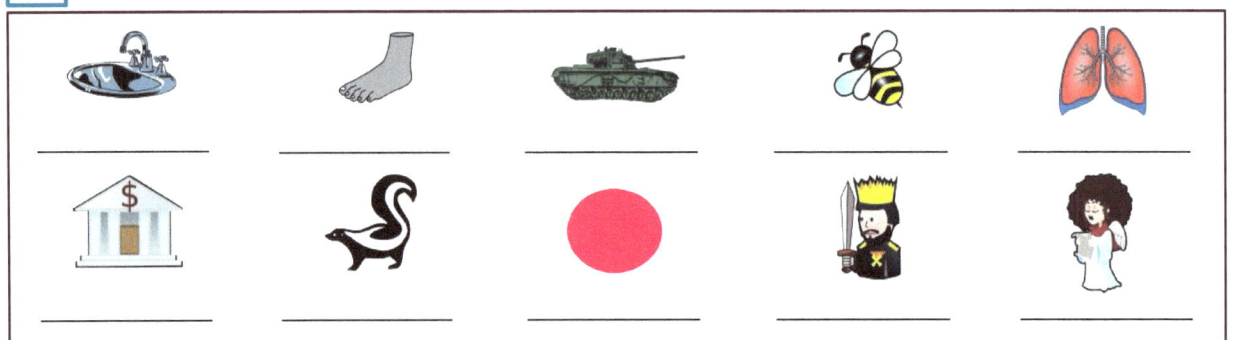

Write sentences with some of the words from above that have double letter endings.

3 COMPLETE
Complete the sentences with the words in the box.

| sting | pink | bank | Jill | small | sing | strong | ball |

1. The circle is color_____.
2. The skunk is _____.
3. I have a new_____account.
4. I have a bee_____on my leg.
5. My friends like to_____.
6. They play with the_____.
7. My father is a _____ man.
8. She is my friend _____.

Lesson 23

4 WRITE
Write the words you learned with each letter ending.

ang   **ing**   **ong**   **ank**   **ink**

1.-_____   1.-_____   1.-_____   1.-_____   1.-_____
2.-_____   2.-_____   2.-_____   2.-_____   2.-_____
3.-_____   3.-_____   3.-_____   3.-_____   3.-_____
4.-_____   4.-_____   4.-_____   4.-_____
               5.-_____   5.-_____   5.-_____

ung

1.-_____

23

Lesson 24

1. R-Controlled Vowels (24.1)

R-Controlled vowels are vowels followed by the letter R.

Read the words. Underline the special sounds.

AR   OR/OAR   IR   ER   UR

AR	OR/OAR	IR	ER	UR
star	horse	stir	her	fur
start	force	bird	verse	curl
scarf	corn	first	fern	turn
far	horn	skirt	term	curve
jar	born	sir		nurse
scar	Lord	dirt		curse
barn	store	birth		burn
park	more			hurt
yarn	board			
farm	short			
shark	fork			
art	form			
	sort			

> IR, ER, OR have the special sound 'ER'.

2. One or Two Consonants

When small words have the combinations of 'vowel + R' followed by one or two consonants as the word ending, you will hear the sound of the R-Controlled vowels.

TERM   GIRL   CORN   FERN   SCARF
FIRST   SKIRT   STORM   SMART   START
STARCH   BIRTH

TERM (one consonant)   FIRST (two consonants)

3. W + R Controlled Vowels (24.2)

W + 'AR' will sound 'OR'. e.g.
WAR   WARM   WARN

W + 'OR' will sound 'ER'. e.g.
WORD   WORK   WORM   WORST
WORLD

The vowel 'A' is silent in the following examples, leaving the 'ER' to be heard.

EARLY   EARN   LEARN   BEAR

EARLY   EARN

Homework: Practice writing the words.

4. Special Sounds (24.3)

When there are 2 vowels together before the letter R, the first vowel is long and the second vowel is silent.

DEAR   FEAR   HAIR   TEAR   STAIRS
BEER   HEAR

DEAR   HAIR

5. R-Controlled Vowels Vs. Silent 'E'

In small words that have a vowel followed by the ending 'RE'. The 'E' at the end of the word is silent and the first vowel in the word will be long. e.g.

CARE   HERE   FIRE   TIRE   CURE

TIRE   CURE

6. R-Controlled Vowels + 'VE'

When small words have the combinations of Vowel + 'R', and are followed by the letter V, the word will always have a letter 'E' at the end.
The letter 'E' will be silent and does not affect the sound of the vowel + 'R'

SERVE   CURVE   STARVE   CARVE
CURVE   SERVE

Dictation

1.- _____   9.- _____
2.- _____   10. _____
3.- _____   11. _____
4.- _____   12. _____
5.- _____   13. _____
6.- _____   14. _____
7.- _____   15. _____
8.- _____   16. _____

Homework: Write sentences using the words.

At Home

Lesson 25

Special Sounds

1 Label the pictures.

_____ _____ _____

GOD
_____ _____ _____

_____ _____ _____

_____ _____ _____

_____ _____ _____

_____ _____ _____

_____ _____ _____

2 WRITING
Write sentences with words that have R-Controlled Vowels.

1._____
2._____
3._____
4._____
5._____
6._____

3 🎧 25.3 READ

DEAR	CARE	TIRE	TERM	STORE
FEAR	HAIR	TEAR	STAIRS	BEER
GIRL	SKIRT	HEAR	CURE	SCORE
AIR	WARM	EARLY	BEAR	SMART
WORD	WORSE	EARN	LEARN	SCARF

4 Write words with each letter ending.

AR
1._____
2._____
3._____
4._____
5._____
6._____
7._____
8._____
9._____
10._____
11._____

OR/OAR
1._____
2._____
3._____
4._____
5._____
6._____
7._____
8._____
9._____
10._____
11._____

IR
1.-_____
2.-_____
3.-_____
4.-_____
5.-_____
6.-_____
7.-_____

ER
1.-_____
2.-_____
3.-_____
4.-_____

UR
1.-_____
2.-_____
3.-_____
4.-_____
5.-_____
6.-_____
7.-_____
8.-_____

Lesson 26

1 CONTRACTIONS

Contraction means to reduce or shorten. We use an apostrophe to show that a letter or letters are left out. e.g. Let us.. let's

The apostrophe has to be placed in a word at the exact point where the letter or letters are omitted.

Two words	Contraction	Two words	Contraction
are not	aren't	could not	couldn't
did not	didn't	should not	shouldn't
can not	can't	I would	I'd
do not	don't	let us	let's
does not	doesn't	she will	she'll
has not	hasn't	there is	there's
have not	haven't	they will	they'll
he is	he's	was not	wasn't
I am	I'm	we are	we're
is not	isn't	were not	weren't
it is	it's	who is	who's
it will	it'll	will not	won't
he will	he'll	you are	you're

2 COMMON WORDS LIST 7

Underline the common words you find in the sentences.

would	could	follow	kind	add
should	must	picture	went	any
world	learn	animal	island	try
great	find	who	love	go

1. You should follow his instructions!
2. I must take a good picture of the baby.
3. What would you like to eat?
4. There aren't any animals in this island.
5. I love to travel around the world.
6. Where should we go for vacations?
7. I'm not sure if I should call him.
8. Would you like to eat fish?
9. They all went to the party.
10. Do you know who called you?
11. You must do your homework every day.
12. Why do you want to learn English?
13. Who wants to learn English?
14. You must study every day.
15. Please follow me to the store.
16. This island is a nice place to live.

3 WRITING

Write sentences with Common words List 7.

1.-_____
2.-_____
3.-_____
4.-_____
5.-_____
6.-_____
7.-_____

Matthew 2:1-3

Jesus was born in the town of Bethlehem in Judea during the time when Herod was king. After Jesus was born, some wise men from the east came to Jerusalem. They followed the star that showed where he was born and went to worship him.

Answer :
1.- Where was Jesus born?
2.- Who came to visit him?

Lesson 27

At Home

CONTRACTIONS

Contraction means:_____.
To write a contraction we use an _____.

1 WRITING
Write the contraction for the two words.

Two words	Contraction	Two words	Contraction
are not	_____	could not	_____
did not	_____	should not	_____
can not	_____	I would	_____
do not	_____	let us	_____
does not	_____	she will	_____
has not	_____	there is	_____
have not	_____	they will	_____
he is	_____	was not	_____
I am	_____	we are	_____
is not	_____	were not	_____
it is	_____	who is	_____
it will	_____	will not	_____
he will	_____	you are	_____

2 READING PRACTICE (27.2)
Underline the contractions you find.

1.- I can't stop the car now. We aren't there yet.
2.- I'm not at home yet. I'll call you later.
3.- Let's go home! You're not doing anything here.
4.- There's not a raindrop to be seen!
5.- Teresa doesn't want to go to the Mall.
6.- I couldn't see my friend at school today.
7.- You don't have flowers in your garden.
8.- The dog doesn't like to bury the bone in the mud.
9.- Who's at the door? It's your friend Claudia.
10.-They aren't busy at home.

4 Write the two words for each contraction.

Contraction	Two words
you'll	_____
she's	_____
he's	_____
we'll	_____
couldn't	_____
shouldn't	_____
I'd	_____
let's	_____
she'll	_____
there's	_____
they'll	_____
wasn't	_____
we're	_____
weren't	_____
who's	_____
won't	_____
you're	_____
It's	_____
hasn't	_____
haven't	_____
isn't	_____
can't	_____
don't	_____
didn't	_____
aren't	_____
they're	_____
I'm	_____
I'll	_____
He'll	_____

Homework: Practice writing contractions correctly. Write sentences using contractions.

3 Find the two words that make each contraction in exercise 2. Rewrite the sentences on the lines provided using the two words instead of the contraction.

1.-_____
2.-_____
3.-_____
4.-_____
5.-_____
6.-_____
7.-_____
8.-_____

Lesson 28

LONG VOWEL SOUNDS

The name of the vowel is the "long vowel sound."

1.- AN ONLY VOWEL: When a vowel stands alone, it is long.

| BE | SO | GO | WE | NO | I |

2. THE SILENT E SKILL: When the small words end with vowel 'E', the 'E' is silent and makes the first vowel in the word long.

GLAD	GLADE		FAT	FATE		RIP	RIPE
CAP	CAPE		SAM	SAME		HOP	HOPE
CAN	CANE		MAD	MADE		SPIN	SPINE
PIN	PINE		FIN	FINE		NOT	NOTE

3. LONG A:

Vowel 'A' is long when it is at the beginning of a small word and there is a silent 'E' at the end.

MAKE	TAKE		FLAME	FAME		CAPE	GAVE
GRAPE	SLAVE		SKATE	LAKE		CRATE	FAKE
MADE	SALE		LATE	STATE		PLACE	SAME
MATE	NAME		PLATE	BLAME		CAGE	GATE

4. LONG I:

Vowel 'i' is long when it is at the beginning of the word and there is a silent 'E' at the end.

MIKE	LIKE		TIME	DIME		RIPE	MICE
STRIKE	MINE		PIPE	WIFE		SIZE	SPRITE
SLIDE	BITE		RIDE	SPINE		KITE	LIFE
NINE	PINE		SIDE	PRICE		DIVE	LIME

Homework: Practice writing the words.
Listen and repeat the words at home.

Dictation

1. _____
2. _____
3. _____
4. _____
5. _____
6. _____
7. _____
8. _____
9. _____
10. _____
11. _____
12. _____
13. _____
14. _____
15. _____
16. _____
17. _____
18. _____
19. _____
20. _____
21. _____

Lesson 29

At Home

1. 🎧 29.1 LISTEN AND ANSWER

Reference to Luke 2 : 41

When Jesus was twelve years old, they went to Jerusalem as usual. While his parents returned home, the boy Jesus stayed behind, but they did not know about it. After three days they found him in the Temple with the religious teachers, listening and asking them questions. Everyone who heard him was amazed at his understanding and wise answers.

When his parents saw him, Jesus said to them, "Why did you look for me? I must be where my Father's work is."

Complete :

When _____ was _____ years old, he stayed behind in _____. His _____ did not know about it.
After _____ days they found him in the _____ with the religious _____, listening and asking questions.

| twelve | parents | teachers | Jerusalem |
| Jesus | three | temple | |

2. 🎧 29.2 Read the words. Mark the long sounds.

MAKE	NOTE	WIFE	RIPE	LINE	SALE	FINE	HOPE
LAKE	PLATE	RIDE	CANE	KITE	LIKE	MINE	SAFE
SIDE	NINE	DIVE	MICE	PINE	SITE	BITE	GAVE
TAKE	SAME	SPINE	WAVE	WHALE	HOME	STONE	PASTE

3. Label the pictures.

_____ _____ _____ _____ _____

_____ _____ _____ _____ _____

UNIT 3

INTRODUCTION

In this unit, you will learn more common words and some words with long 'o, u, and e' sounds. You will practice writing and using words with 'k, ck, sk, and c'.

Later, you will identify and read words with soft 'c' and hard 'c' sounds and will practice using them correctly in sentences.

You will also practice reading sentences and Bible scriptures.

OBJECTIVES

- Learn more common words.
- Read words with long vowel sounds.
- Read and write words with 'k, ck, sk, and c'.
- Identify words with soft and hard 'C' sound.
- Read sentences and Bible scriptures.
- Write sentences.

Lesson 30

1. LONG O:

Vowel 'O' is long when it is at the beginning of a one small Word. The 'E' at the end is silent.

 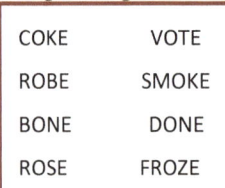

o_e

COKE	VOTE	TONE	STONE	ROLE	STOLE
ROBE	SMOKE	POPE	HOPE	NOSE	ZONE
BONE	DONE	ROPE	ROME	HOLE	CONE
ROSE	FROZE	COPE	JOKE	POLE	HOME

2. LONG U:

Vowel 'U' is long when it is at the beginning of a one small Word. The 'E' at the end is silent.

 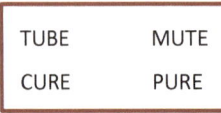

u_e

TUBE	MUTE	CUTE	MULE	USE	FLUTE
CURE	PURE	HUGE	CUBE		

Vowel 'U' is long when it has the vowel combination 'ue'. The 'e' at the end is silent.

 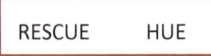

ue

RESCUE	HUE	CONTINUE	DUE	VALUE	ARGUE

ew

STEW	FEW	CHEW	NEW	JEWEL	DEW

Homework: Practice reading and writing the words.
Write sentences using the words.

DICTATION

1._____   5._____   9._____   13._____
2._____   6._____   10._____   14._____
3._____   7._____   11._____   15._____
4._____   8._____   12._____   16._____

1 LABEL THE PICTURES.

2 COMMON WORDS LIST 8

Underline the common words you find in the sentences.

people	down	take	place	part
after	little	year	show	live
every	good	made	get	plant
study	school	grow	artist	branch

1.- Many people grow plants in their yards.
2.- They live in a small house down the street.
3.- I made a trip to Europe last year.
4.- I have to study to get good grades at school.
5.- A talent show is taking place at school right now.
6.- He is a good friend. He visits me every month.
7.- This year I want to go to The United States.
8.- What place would you like to visit next year?
9.- My plants grow very fast.
10. Did you take my book? I need it at school.
11. Please show me the new branch of the plant.
12. She wants to be a good artist.

Homework: Practice reading and writing sentences.

Lesson 31

At Home

1 SENTENCES
Complete the sentences with the words in the box.

| nose | cute | huge | hope | smoke | coke | pure | flute |

1. My eyes are big. My _____ is small.
2. We have love, faith, and _____.
3. I do not drink _____, only water.
4. The girl plays the _____ very well.
5. It is bad to _____ cigarettes.
6. That is a _____ palace.
7. The baby girl is so _____!
8. I need to have a _____ heart.

2 Read the words. Mark the long sounds.

CHEW	BONE	HUGE	TUBE	FLUTE	JOKE	NEW	CONE
ROPE	TONE	STOVE	NOSE	FEW	COKE	STONE	ROME
VOTE	STONE	CUTE	MULE	PURE	CURE	SMOKE	VALUE

3 WRITING
Write sentences with words that have long 'O' and long 'U' sounds.

1. _____
2. _____
3. _____
4. _____
5. _____
6. _____

4 Write the missing letter or letters to form a word with long 'o' or long 'u' sound.

1.- c__k__	5.- p__r__	9. je____l	13. ch____	17. v__t__
2.- st__n__	6.- val____	10. arg____	14. m__l__	18. sm__k__
3.- c__t__	7.- fl__t__	11. h__m__	15. resc____	19. h__l__
4.- h__g__	8.- contin____	12. r__p__	16. vi____	20. __s__

5 Write the letter 'O' on the line provided if the word has the long 'o' sound.
Write the letter 'U' if the word has a long 'u' sound.

argue ____	tone ____	role ____	cute ____	bone ____	value ____
vote ____	stone ____	nose ____	tube ____	pure ____	hole ____
rescue ____	pope ____	few ____	rose ____	new ____	use ____
smoke ____	chew ____	pole ____	flute ____	cube ____	cure ____

Lesson 31.1

7. LONG E: Listen. Read. Mark the long 'e' sounds for each word.

1. **Vowel 'E' is long when it is followed by the vowel 'A' at the beginning of the word and there is a silent 'E' at the end.**

LEAGUE	LEAVE
GREASE	PLEASE

EAGLE	TEASE
TEASE	PEACE

BREATHE

2. **Vowel 'E' is long in one syllable words that have the two vowels 'ea' together.**

EACH	TEAM
TEACH	TEA
SEA	LEAK
DREAM	CREAM

BLEACH	LEAD
CHEAP	LEASH
REACH	READ
EAST	BEAST

SEAT	NEAT
REAL	HEAT
PEACH	LEAF
MEAL	MEAT

There are also some two syllable words that have the vowel combination 'ea'. The letter 'E' has a long sound and the letter 'A' is silent. e.g. REASON, SEASON, EASEL, BEAVER.

3. **Vowel 'E' has a long sound in the combination of the vowels 'ee'.**

SHEEP	MEET
SEEK	WEEK
QUEEN	SEED

NEED	SEEN
SPEED	BEE
SPEECH	PEEL

AGREE	HEEL
THREE	DEEP
CHEEK	BEER

LONG E:

4. Vowel 'E' has a long sound if followed by a consonant. The 'E' at the end of the Word is silent.

CHINESE	GENE
ATHLETE	THEME

DELETE	THESE
ADHERE	HERE

EXTREME	PETE
	SCENE

5. When 'ie' are together and there is a silent 'E' at the end of the word, vowels 'ie' have a long 'E' sound.

ACHIEVE	PIECE
BELIEVE	NIECE

RETRIEVE	GRIEVE
FIERCE	

PIERCE

6. **The vowels 'ie' together have the sound 'i'.**

BRIEFCASE	BRIEF
CASHIER	PRIEST

COOKIE	CHIEF
CALORIE	DIESEL

FIELD	
RELIEF	MOVIE

Dictation   Homework: Practice reading and writing the words..

1.- _____	6.- _____	11. _____	16. _____
2.- _____	7.- _____	12. _____	17. _____
3.- _____	8.- _____	13. _____	18. _____
4.- _____	9.- _____	14. _____	19. _____
5.- _____	10. _____	15. _____	20. _____

Lesson 31.2

At Home

1 Label the pictures.

_____ _____ _____ _____ _____

_____ _____ _____ _____ _____

_____ _____ _____ _____ _____

2 Complete the sentences with the words from the box.

THREE	EASEL	SPEECH	PRIEST	BEES	LEAGUE	CASHIER
TEA	SEASON	READ	TEAM	PLEASE	SEAT	

1.- This _____, our soccer _____ will play in the mayor _____.
2.- My friends _____ a book about honey _____ in Science class.
3.- May I have a cup of hot _____ _____?
4.- The painter is using his new _____ to paint.
5.- John's new car has a nice leader _____.
6.- The _____ gave us a nice _____ about moral values.
7.- She has worked as a _____ at the restaurant for _____ months.

3 Write the missing letter or letters to each word with long 'E' sound.

1.- extr__m__	5.- gr__ __v__	9. h__ __t	13. athl__t__	17. __ __ch
2.- __ __s__l	6.- sp__ __d	10. l__ __f	14. d__ __p	18. l__ __k
3.- bl__ __ch	7.- calor__ __	11. r__ __ch	15. s__ __	19. p__ __ch
4.- mov__ __	8.- del__t__	12. p__ __c__	16. t__ __	20. s__ __son

Lesson 32

🎧 32.1 'K', 'CK', 'SK', OR 'C'?

When the word has one syllable:

K is used with the silent 'E' skill.

| TAKE | MAKE | LAKE | LIKE | BIKE |

K is used after the letters 'N' and 'L'

| MILK | SILK | PINK | SINK | LINK |

K is used after a vowel digraph (ee, ea)

| BREAK | PEAK | SEAK | SEEK | BEAK |

K is used after vowel + R.

| BARK | DARK | CORK | WORK | PERK |

K is used before vowels 'E', 'I', or 'Y'

| KEPT | KID | MILKY | KIT |

SK 🎧 32.2 are used to start or end a word.

ASK	RISK	MASK	BASKET
DESK	DISK	DUSK	SKETCH	SKILL
SKIP	SKULL	SKIRT	TASK

SK are used before vowels 'E', 'I', or 'Y' at the beginning of the words.

| SKY | SKETCH | SKI | SKIRT | SKIP |

C starts a word when followed by vowels a, o, u.

| CAT | CAP | COME | COST | CURL |

CK are used after short vowel sounds

SICK	CLOCK	SACK	DUCK	NECK
BLACK	BLOCK	BACK	BRICK	TRICK
TRACK	DOCK	SOCK	ROCK	PACK

Homework: Practice reading and writing the words. Learn the rules to use 'k', 'ck', 'sk', 'c'.

1 🎧 32.3 READING PRACTICE
Listen and repeat the sentences.

1. They like to drink milk.
2. Did you speak to Mike?
3. Did you know that he speaks English very well?
4. Blake, do you work by the lake?
5. The girl's toy is pink.
6. Ducks do not learn tricks.
7. The dog barks at the black duck.
8. Mike likes his new bike. It is dark blue.
9. Did you take the clock from the black table?
10. My friend Jake is sick. He has a pain in his neck.
11. My uncle Carlos got a new clock for the wall.
12. Mark! Ducks do not drink milk! They eat corn.

Circle the words that have the sounds of 'k'.

2 DICTATION
Write the sentences you hear.

1.-_____
2.-_____
3.-_____
4.-_____

Dictation

1._____	13._____
2._____	14._____
3._____	15._____
4._____	16._____
5._____	17._____
6._____	18._____
7._____	19._____
8._____	20._____
9._____	21._____
10._____	22._____
11._____	23._____
12._____	24._____

Lesson **33**

At Home

1 🎧 **LISTEN**

Listen to the Scripture. Then, answer the questions.

Reference to Luke 3:2-6

John, the son of Zechariah, was living in the desert, and he began to preach the message he received from God. He told the people to be baptized to show that they wanted to change their lives, and then their sins would be forgiven.

1.- Who is the son of Zechariah?
2.- What did John tell the people to do?

WORDS WITH K, CK, SK, OR C

2 **LABEL THE PICTURES**

_____ _____ _____ _____ _____

_____ _____ _____ _____ _____

_____ _____ _____ _____ _____

3 **PRACTICE**
Write the missing letter or letters.

1. ta ____   9. do ____   19. ____ill
2. la ____   10. smo ____   20. ____irt
3. ma ____   11. pee ____   21. ____ull
4. ra ____   12. see ____   22. ____etch
5. wor ____   13. brea ____   23. ____st
6. pin ____   14. blo ____   24. a____
7. du ____   15. bla ____   25. ____ome
8. li ____   16. per ____   26. ____id

5 **Unscramble**
Unscramble the words.
Write the correct word on the line provided.

1. klis _____   6. olkcc _____
2. tkecsh _____ 7. iymlk _____
3. tksbae _____ 8. rowk _____
4. moce _____   9. epkr _____
5. lckob _____ 10. kibe _____

6 **word search**
Find the 10 hidden words.

```
b n s k y a b p s e t
r e x h a u i t e d b
i s t r o c k r i m v
c k c n e l e i p y d
k i u r u s t c o m e
s l r y s l o k e d p
m l l i l t b r e a k
```
_____
_____
_____
_____
_____
_____
_____
_____
_____
_____

4 Circle the letter or letters that stand for the sounds of 'k', 'ck', 'sk', or 'c'.

bark	milk	ask	cat
dark	silk	risk	come
kept	pink	disk	cost

Lesson 34

 ## SOFT 'C'

Letter 'C' has the sound of 'S' when it is followed by the vowels 'e, i,' or 'y'.

CE

CENT	CELERY	RECESS	BALANCE	PRINCE	CENTIMETER	CELL
SILENCE	NOTICE	SERVICE	DISTANCE	DANCE	ANCESTOR	FENCE
FRANCE	JUICE	PEACE	LICENSE	SINCE	ADVANCE	ONCE

CI

CINDER	SPECIAL	CIVIL	SPECIFIC	PENCIL	ACID	CIRCUS
CIRCUIT	PACIFIC	RECITE	EXCITE	DECIDE	CITY	CIRCLE

CY

LUCY	AGENCY	JUICY	ICY	FANCY	VACANCY	BICYCLE
CYLINDER	CYMBAL	FANCY	MERCY	BOUNCY	DELEGACY	EMERGENCY

FACE	TWICE	GRACE	PEACE	SPICE	PRICE	NICE	LICE
MICE	TRACE	ICE	RICE	SPACE	PLACE	RACE	DICE

Words ending in 'CE' that have only one vowel before it, have a silent 'E' at the end of the word.
The first vowel in the word is long.

Homework: Practice reading and writing the words.
Write sentences using words with soft C.

1 Label the pictures.

 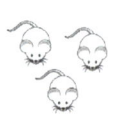   
_____ _____ _____ _____ _____

_____ _____ _____ _____ _____

2 READING PRACTICE

Circle the words that have a soft 'C' sound.

1. Have you ever been to France, Cindy?
2. Cid will dance with Lucy.
3. Do you want an icy cup of tea?
4. Cindy is her Dad's princess.
5. Mice are not nice! I saw three mice once.
6. Let's go to your place for an orange juice.
7. I was at that fancy place twice.
8. There was a prize for the man who won the race.
9. Did he paint the complete fence?
10. He eats a delicious celery and a carrot during recess time.
11. I like to see her face. She looks very nice.
12. What is the distance from here to the city?
13. Do I need a special license to drive a motorcycle?
14. There is a vacancy to work in that circus.

Dictation

1. _____ 11. _____
2. _____ 12. _____
3. _____ 13. _____
4. _____ 14. _____
5. _____ 15. _____
6. _____ 16. _____
7. _____ 17. _____
8. _____ 18. _____
9. _____ 19. _____
10. _____ 20. _____

Lesson 35

HARD 'C'

When 'C' stands with vowels 'a, o, u', it has the sound of 'K'.

CA	CAT	CAMERA	CARROT	SCAN	CABIN	CAB	CAP
	CALL	CARRY	CASINO	CAR	CAMEL	CAN'T	CAN

CO	COME	CORRECT	COMET	COUSIN	COIN	COMMAND

CU	CURTAIN	CUT	CUSTOM	CURVE	CURL	CURLY	CURSE

CUTE	CABLE	CAKE	CANE	CAVE	COKE	CODE	CURE

When there is a one syllable word ending in letter 'E', the 'E' is silent and the first vowel has the long sound.

1 Label the pictures.

2 READING PRACTICE

Circle the words that have a hard 'C' sound.

1. I'd like a piece of that chocolate cake!
2. Carol has a nice picture of a camel in the desert.
3. Do you want to eat chocolate cake?
4. That road has many curves.
5. Can you please find the code on this can of corn?
6. I like the color of my new curtains.
7. Carmen's baby has curly hair.
8. Please buy some candy canes for Christmas.
9. I will buy a new camera for the camping trip.
10. Carlos is a cute baby boy!

Dictation

1._____ 11._____
2._____ 12._____
3._____ 13._____
4._____ 14._____
5._____ 15._____
6._____ 16._____
7._____ 17._____
8._____ 18._____
9._____ 19._____
10._____ 20._____

Homework: Practice writing words with 'C' sounds. Learn the rules to use the words in sentences.

4 WRITING

Write sentences with the new words you learned.

1. _____
2. _____
3. _____
4. _____
5. _____
6. _____

At Home   Lesson 36

HARD AND SOFT 'C' SOUND

1 Read the words. Circle the letter or letters that make the soft 'C' sound. Write the letters on the line next to each word.

CENT _____	PACIFIC _____	NOTICE _____	TWICE _____
JUICY _____	CELERY _____	CINDER _____	PRINCE _____
CYCLE _____	RECENT _____	SERVICE _____	DANCE _____
FENCE _____	CELL _____	LUCY _____	AGENCY _____
RECESS _____	CIVIL _____	NICE _____	ONCE _____
EXCITE _____	PRICE _____	MICE _____	FRANCE _____
LICENSE _____	SILENCE _____	SERVICE _____	SPACE _____

2 Circle the letter or letters that make the 'c' sound. Write letter 'S' if the sound is soft or letter 'H' if the sound is hard.

CODE _____	TRACE _____	SCAN _____
CAT _____	CENTIMETER _____	DECIDE _____
CAMERA _____	PEACE _____	COMET _____
SCAN _____	CARRY _____	CELL _____
CARROT _____	CIRCUS _____	CODE _____
CAMELEON _____	CALL _____	FENCE _____
CABIN _____	ACID _____	CAME _____
CAMEL _____	CABLE _____	CITY _____
AGENCY _____	PLACE _____	ICE _____
COKE _____	CURSE _____	CAKE _____
CAVE _____	CANE _____	COAT _____
CYLINDER _____	PRINCE _____	CURE _____

3 Unscramble
Unscramble the words. Write the correct answer on the line provided.

1. psifceci _____
2. edcdei _____
3. leciybc _____
4. iecl _____
5. vcae _____
6. cynbuo _____
7. cdlgeeya _____
8. nictura _____
9. stcomu _____
10. tcaror _____
11. lmace _____

UNIT 4

INTRODUCTION

In this unit, you will learn more common words. You will be able to identify soft 'G' and hard 'G' sounds in words and practice the use of those words in sentences.

Later, you will practice the use of consonant digraphs are as well as some words with them. You will use some word endings and adjacent vowels. You will also identify 'ou/ow' and 'au/aw' sounds in words.

Finally, you will continue to practice reading and writing sentences as well as reading Bible scriptures.

OBJECTIVES

- Learn more common words.
- Identify words with soft 'G' and hard 'G' sound.
- Learn words with consonant digraphs.
- Learn words with 'dge' endings.
- Learn words with adjacent vowels.
- Identify 'OU/OW' sounds in words.
- Identify 'AU/AW' sounds in words.
- Practice reading sentences and Bible scriptures.
- Take dictation of sentences and write sentences.

Lesson 37

🎧 37.1 SOFT 'G'

When 'G' stands with vowels 'e, I, or y', it has the sound of 'J'.

GE	GEM	GENTLE	GENEROUS	ORANGE	GENT	GEOGRAPHY	BADGE
GI	MAGIC	ENGINE	GIANT	ORIGINAL	RIGID	DIGITAL	GIRAFFE
GY	GYM	APOLOGY	ENERGY	ALLERGY	ANALOGY	BIOLOGY	
CĀGE (ch)	RANGE	CAGE	GENE	STAGE	AGE	PAGE	HUGE

When the one syllable words end 'GE', 'GE' will have the sound 'ch' and the first vowel in the word will have a long sound. When 'GE' is at the beginning of the word and there is a silent 'E' at the end, the 'G' has a soft sound as in GENE.

1 LABEL THE PICTURES

When there is a one syllable word ending in the letter 'E', the 'E' is silent and the first vowel has the long sound.

2 🎧 37.2 READING PRACTICE

Listen and answer the questions.

Reference to Luke 3:7

John baptized many people. But he said to them, "Change your hearts! And show by your lives that you have changed."

Answer:

1.- Who baptized the people?

2.- What good fruit can we produce in our lives?

Dictation

1._____ 10._____
2._____ 11._____
3._____ 12._____
4._____ 13._____
5._____ 14._____
6._____ 15._____
7._____ 16._____
8._____ 17._____
9._____ 18._____

Homework: Practice reading and writing words with 'G sounds.

Lesson 38

🎧 38.1 HARD 'G'

When 'G' is followed by the vowels 'a, o, u', it has the sound of 'G' as in 'get'.

GA | GAS GALAXY GALLERY GALLON GANG GARAGE GARBAGE GARLIC

GO | GOLDEN GO GOLF GOAT GORILLA GOSSIP GOD GOVERNOR

GU | GUM GUARANTEE GUN GUARD GUEST REGULAR GUESS

GAME | GATE GAVE GAZE GAME GRACE

1 READING PRACTICE 🎧 38.2

Underline the words with soft 'G' sound.
Circle the words that have hard 'G' sound.

1. My generous friend gave me a nice gift.
2. I have a golden ring for my mom.
3. I love God.
4. They are in a good Science group.
5. They study the galaxy.
6. Let's go to your place today..
7. Do you want some more gum?
8. Gossip is not good.
9. Gustavo is a security guard.
10. Where did he go? Can you guess?
11. I do not like garlic.
12. Who gave you the golf set?
13. Is that green paint for the gate?
14. I like goats but I do not like gorillas.

Homework: Practice reading and writing sentences. Write your own sentences with words that have 'G' sound.

2 WRITING

Write sentences with words that have a G sound. Circle the words in the sentences.

1._____
2._____
3._____
4._____
5._____
6._____
7._____

Dictation

1._____ 7._____
2._____ 8._____
3._____ 9._____
4._____ 10._____
5._____ 11._____
6._____ 12._____

4 Write the missing letter or letters.

1. ____lic   7. ____rilla   13. ____ography
2. ____llery   8. ____rage   14. bad ____
3. ____te   9. ____lden   15. ____ntle
4. ____me   10. ____rbage   16. sta____
5. ____rd   11. ____raffe   17. ____laxi
6. ____ess   12. ____nerous   18. ____llon

5 COMPLETE

Use the words from the box to complete the scripture.

Reference to Luke 3:7-9

_____ baptized many _____. But he said to _____," Change your _____! And show by your _____ that you have changed."

| people | them | John |
| hearts | | lives |

At Home

Lesson **39**

HARD 'G' AND SOFT 'G' SOUND

1 Label the pictures.

_____ _____ _____ _____ _____

_____ _____ _____ _____ _____

2 **WORD SEARCH**

Find the words with, soft 'G' and hard 'G' sound. Write the words on the lines provided for each sound.

a	g	e	r	p	b	a	d	g	e	g	g
g	e	t	h	a	u	s	i	e	g	u	r
x	n	t	u	g	a	s	g	i	a	m	a
i	t	l	n	e	k	e	i	p	t	e	c
o	l	n	g	i	v	e	t	t	e	d	e
g	e	n	e	u	s	g	a	l	a	x	y
o	r	i	g	i	n	a	l	g	a	m	e
m	t	g	e	o	g	r	a	p	h	y	o

SOFT 'G'   HARD 'G'

_____   _____
_____   _____
_____   _____
_____   _____
_____   _____
_____   _____
_____   _____
_____   _____

3 Write the letter 'S' if the sound is soft or letter 'H' if the sound is hard.

gas ____	geese ____	galaxy ____
gem ____	gene ____	orange ____
cage ____	rigid ____	regular ____
gym ____	gaze ____	golden ____
game ____	gossip ____	generous ____
cage ____	huge ____	giraffe ____
gum ____	giant ____	guard ____
go ____	goat ____	engine ____
golf ____	goose ____	gave ____
gift ____	god ____	gate ____
stage ____	range ____	guess ____
age ____	page ____	gorilla ____

4 **WORD SCRAMBLE**

Unscramble the words.

1. rgdau _____
2. lrgeura _____
3. sugse _____
4. onrvgeor _____
5. clgiar _____
6. mgae _____
7. zgea _____
8. vgae _____
9. tgea _____
10. nug _____
11. ggna _____
12. dirgi _____
13. tago _____
14. niatg _____
15. ghue _____
16. logf _____
17. ftgi _____
18. nogdle _____
19. asteg _____
20. ygm _____

Lesson 40

🎧 3 CONSONANT DIGRAPHS

TCH — If the word is a one syllable word with a short vowel, it will end in the letters 'TCH', if there is no other consonant between the vowel and the 'TCH'.

| CATCH | BATCH | ITCH | HATCH | STITCH | PATCH | FETCH | LATCH | SKETCH |

MATCH   CATCH   WITCH

Exceptions : MUCH, SUCH, COUCH, TOUCH, WHICH, NICHE, RICH

CHL sounds 'kl'
When the letters 'CH' are followed by a letter 'L', they sound 'kl'.
CHLORIDE

CHR sounds 'kr'
When the letters 'CH' are followed by the letter 'R', they sound 'kr'.
CHROME   CHRONIC   CHRIST   CHRISTMAS

SCH sounds 'sk'
When the letters 'CH' have a letter 'S' before them, they sound 'sk'.
SCHOOL   SCHEDULE   SCHEMA   SCHOOLBAG

🎧 3 CONSONANT DIGRAPHS II

SHR sounds 'shrh'
We add the consonant 'R' to form the digraph 'SHR'.
SHRIMP   SHRED   SHRINK

THR sounds 'trh'
We add the consonant 'R' to form the digraph 'THR'.
THROAT   THRUST   THRILL   THREE   THRONE

Dictation
1. _____
2. _____
3. _____
4. _____
5. _____
6. _____
7. _____
8. _____
9. _____
10. _____
11. _____
12. _____
13. _____
14. _____
15. _____

Homework: Practice writing the words.

🎧 Reference to Mark 1:9-13

John baptized Jesus in the Jordan River. As Jesus was coming up out of the water, he saw the sky torn open. The Spirit came down on him like a dove.
A voice came from heaven and said, "You are my Son, the one I love. I am very pleased with you."

Then the Spirit sent Jesus into the desert alone. He was there for 40 days, being tempted by Satan. Then angels came and helped him.

Answer:
1.- Who baptized Jesus?
2.- Where was Jesus baptized?
3.- What happened to the sky?
4. What came down on Jesus?

1.- Where was Jesus taken?
2.- How many days was he there?
3.- Who tempted Jesus?
4. Who came to help Jesus?

Lesson 41

At Home

3 CONSONANT DIGRAPHS

1 Write the words with digraph.

THR	SCH
_____	_____
_____	_____
_____	_____
_____	_____
_____	

TCH	SHR
_____	_____
_____	_____
_____	_____
_____	_____

	CHR
_____	_____
_____	_____
_____	_____
_____	_____

	CHL
	_____

3 Label the pictures.

_____   _____

_____   _____

_____

_____   _____

_____

_____   _____

_____

_____ 3

2 WRITING
Write sentences using words with digraphs.

1.- _____
2.- _____
3.- _____
4.- _____
5.- _____
6.- _____
7.- _____

Lesson 42

42.1 3 CONSONANT DIGRAPHS III

Underline the consonant digraphs.

STR sounds 'strh'

STRESS	STRANGE	STRUCTURE	
STRAW	STRAY	STRETCH	STRING
STRICT	STRING	STREET	TRONG

SPR sounds 'sprh'

SPRAY	SPRITE	SPREAD	SPRING
SPRINKLE			

PHR sounds 'frh'

PHRASE	PHRASAL	PHRENETIC

1 READING PRACTICE

Practice reading the sentences.
1.- I like spring!
2.- Is this a phrasal verb?
3.- He is a stranger.
4.- Do not cross the street now.
5.- How do you say that phrase in English?

Homework: Listen and repeat the words at home.

2 'DGE' Sounds 'dch'

If there is a one syllable word ending in 'DGE', the vowel in the word will have a short sound.

EDGE	JUDGE	BRIDGE	FUDGE	PLEDGE	BUDGE	BUDGET	CARTRIDGE

42.2 Reference to Matthew 4:23-25

Jesus went from place to place telling the good news about God's kingdom. And he healed all the people's diseases and sicknesses.

The people brought to him all those who were sick. They were suffering from different kinds of diseases and pain. Some had demons inside them.

1.- What were people suffering?
2.- Who healed them?
3.- How can we show compassion to people in need or in suffering?

3 42.3 COMMON WORDS LIST 9

Underline the common words you find.

which	time	way	about	write	air
right	set	long	line	move	pay
large	well	mean	turn	think	build

1. I read a book about animals.
2. What do you mean by that?
3. I think this is the way to the Mall.
4. Which is your house?
5. Could you please set the table?
6. I want to build my own house.
7. Could you please turn on the fan?
8. Can you come with me?
9. It is your turn in the line.
10. I will move to Chicago next week.
11. Please write my new address.
12. This music makes me move!
13. I have a new set of paints.
14. There is a long line at the bank.

Dictation

1. _____ 9. _____
2. _____ 10. _____
3. _____ 11. _____
4. _____ 12. _____
5. _____ 13. _____
6. _____ 14. _____
7. _____ 15. _____
8. _____ 16. _____

Lesson 43

At Home

1 Write words with digraphs.

STR
_____
_____
_____
_____
_____
_____

SPR
_____
_____
_____

PHR
_____
_____
_____

2 Write sentences with common words list 9.

| time | write | long | line | large | build |

1. _____
2. _____

3 Circle the words with 3 consonant digraphs.

phrasal	strict	small	spider	string	brother
strong	straw	spray	strong	matter	start
stem	page	practice	spam	better	mother

4 Label the pictures.

_____

_____

_____

_____

_____

What did you learn in Matthew 4:23-25?
_____
_____
_____
_____

5 Write words with 'dge' ending.

DGE
_____ _____
_____ _____
_____ _____

Lesson 44

Adjacent Vowels

 44.1

WHEN 2 VOWELS ARE ADJACENT THE 1ST VOWEL IS LONG AND THE 2ND VOWEL IS SILENT.

ŌA	EE	EA	AI
oak	eel	dream	plain
croak	bleed	deal	train
soak	seed	heat	main
boat	feed	leak	hail
float	feel	mean	claim
boast	heel	meat	maid
roast	feet	neat	paint
toast	seek	read	train
load	see	eat	wait
coal	sweet	beat	snail
coat	sleep	beast	stain
loan	greet	please	trail
toad	seem	sea	tail
road	sweep	seat	mail
	sweet		rain

Mark the sounds in each word.

1 44.2 READING PRACTICE

Circle the words that have adjacent vowels.

1. His green kite is on the tree.
2. There is a leak on the roof.
3. Did you hear the toad croak?
4. I felt the heat of the toaster.
5. That load seems to be big.
6. I want to eat meat.
7. He reads about seeds.
8. I live on Main Street.
9. I have to wait for a mail this week.
10. Please go to sleep.
11. He lives near the sea.
12. I need some food to eat.
13. The maid seems tired.
14. I will paint my boat green.
15. I boast about my new boat.

1.- What have you learned about Jesus?

2.- How can you tell he is the Son of God?

   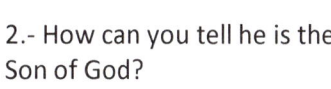 

sounds 'bout'   sounds 'fiit'   sounds 'sit'   sounds 'trein'   sounds 'suit'   sounds 'kout'

Dictation

1. _____ 8. _____ 15. _____
2. _____ 9. _____ 16. _____
3. _____ 10. _____ 17. _____
4. _____ 11. _____ 18. _____
5. _____ 12. _____ 19. _____
6. _____ 13. _____ 20. _____
7. _____ 14. _____ 21. _____

4 DICTATION
Write the sentences you hear from the reading practice.

1.-_____
2.-_____
3.-_____
4.-_____
5.-_____
6.-_____
7.-_____

At Home Lesson **45**

1 Write the words for each adjacent vowel. Then, mark the sounds.

ŌA	ĒE	ĒA	ĀI

2 Label the pictures.

Matthew 5:1–3

When Jesus saw the crowds of people, he went up on a hill and sat down. His followers came and sat next to him. Jesus said,

"Blessed are the ones who know they are spiritually in need. God's kingdom belongs to them."

1.- What did Jesus talk about to the people?

49

Lesson 46

46.1 More Adjacent Vowels

OE   IE   UI

Joe	pie	suit
toe	tie	fruit
foe	lie	
hoe	die	
doe		

Mark the sounds in each word.

JOE — sounds 'iou'
PIE — sounds 'pai'
DIE — sounds 'dai'

1 46.2 READING PRACTICE
Circle the words that have adjacent vowels.

1. Oscar has a new suit.
2. He needs a new tie for his suit.
3. Joe is my best friend at church.
4. God doesn't like us to tell lies.
5. Water your plant or it will die.
6. I can not bake apple pies.
7. He needs a hoe to work the land.
8. The soldiers fight against their foe.
9. I think deer are beautiful.
10. What kind of fruit do you like?
11. I hurt my toe with that hoe!

Homework: Listen and repeat the sentences at home.

2 46.4 Listen and mark the sounds in each word.

TRIED	PAIR	HAIR	HEAR	DEAR	TEAR	NEAR
DEAR	ROAST	CHAIN	BRAIN	TRAIN	BEE	AFRAID
KNEE	TEA	RAISE	OBTAIN	BAY	PAIN	MAIN

When small words end in the sound of 'k', the vowel is long. The word will end in the letters 'ke'.

46.3 Matthew 5:4-8

Jesus said, "Blessed are those who are sad now. God will comfort them.

Blessed are those who are humble.
They will be given the land God promised.

Blessed are those who want to do right more than anything else. God will fully satisfy them.

Blessed are those who show mercy to others. Mercy will be given to them.

Blessed are those whose thoughts are pure. They will be with God."

Answer:

1.- Who is talking?
2.- Who are blessed?
3.- Are you humble?
4.- Do you show mercy to others?

Dictation

1. _____ 11. _____
2. _____ 12. _____
3. _____ 13. _____
4. _____ 14. _____
5. _____ 15. _____
6. _____ 16. _____
7. _____ 17. _____
8. _____ 18. _____
9. _____ 19. _____
10. _____ 20. _____

Lesson 47

At Home

1. Complete the Scripture.

Matthew 5:1–8

- Great blessings belong to those who know they are spiritually in _____. God's kingdom belongs to them.
- Blessed are those who are _____ now. God will _____ them.
- Blessed are those who are _____. They will be given the _____ God promised.
- Blessed are those who want to do _____ more than anything else.
- God will fully _____ them.
- Blessed are those who show _____ to others. Mercy will be given to them.
- Blessed are those whose thoughts are _____. They will be with _____.

RIGHT
NEED
HUMBLE
PURE
SAD
SATISFY
GOD
MERCY
LAND
COMFORT

Answer:
1. Who will comfort the sad?
2. What are some right things we could do?
3.- How can we show mercy to others?

2. More Adjacent Vowels

Write the words for each pair of adjacent vowels, Then, mark the sounds in each word.

OE̸   I̸E̸   UI̸

3. WRITING

Write sentences using words with adjacent vowels.

1. _____
2. _____
3. _____
4. _____
5. _____
6. _____

4. Unscramble

Unscramble the words in the box.

1. esped _____
2. ebtas _____
3. dare _____
4. mial _____
5. lpina _____
6. tbao _____
7. aset _____
8. ltia _____
9. ocakr _____
10. tsewe _____
11. esed _____
12. arod _____
13. doat _____
14. teef _____
15. itpan _____
16. tnae _____
17. ngari _____
18. insla _____
19. naol _____
20. tolaf _____

Lesson 48

WORDS WITH 'OU / OW'

These two letter combinations sound 'au'. The 'W' sounds like a vowel.

OU

COMPOUND	AMOUNT	ACCOUNT	ALOUD	GROUND	ABOUT	FOUND
FOUNTAIN	AROUND	BOUNCE	HOUSE	BLOUSE	MOUSE	CLOUD
MOUNTAIN	COUNT	SOUTH	OUCH	ROUND	OUT	SOUND

OW

DOWN	TOWN	CROWN	HOW	BROWNIE	BROWN	CLOWN
ALLOW	FLOWER	TOWER	COW	DROWN	FROWN	NOW

*OW

BORROW	LOW	SLOW	BLOW	NARROW	GROW	GLOW
ARROW	BOW	BELOW	ELBOW	FOLLOW	FLOW	ROW

* In this case 'OW' sounds 'ou'.

Homework: Practice reading and writing the words.

1. Reading Practice

Circle the words with OU/OW sounds.

1. That garden has a water fountain!
2. His house is near the mountain.
3. The clown is so funny!
4. My sister has a new blouse.
5. The balls bounce very well.
6. The turtle is slow.
7. Please follow directions!
8. My sister hurt her elbow.
9. My mother bakes brownies.
10. There is a mouse in my house!
11. That castle has a tower.
12. He has a bow and arrows for the game.
13. The farmer has many cows.
14. What is the book about?

Homework: Practice reading and writing sentences.

Dictation

1. _____ 13. _____
2. _____ 14. _____
3. _____ 15. _____
4. _____ 16. _____
5. _____ 17. _____
6. _____ 18. _____
7. _____ 19. _____
8. _____ 20. _____
9. _____ 21. _____
10. _____ 22. _____
11. _____ 23. _____
12. _____ 24. _____

Homework: Practice reading and writing the words.

Matthew 5:9-10

Great blessings belong to those who work to bring peace. God will call them his sons and daughters. Great blessings belong to those who suffer persecution for doing what is right. God's kingdom belongs to them.

Write the missing word

Great _____ belong to those who_____ to bring _____. _____ will call them his _____ and _____.

Lesson 49

WORDS WITH 'AU / AW'

In this combination, 'W' becomes a vowel. These two vowels together have a special sound 'O', as in SAW.

AU

| PAUL | AUDITORY | FRAUD | APPLAUD | ASTRONAUT | ASSAULT | AUCTION |
| AUNT | AUTHOR | AUGUST | AUTHENTIC | AUTUMN | | |

AW

| HAWK | SAW | DRAW | CLAW | STRAW | AWESOME | CRAWL | PAW |

Dictation

1. _____
2. _____
3. _____
4. _____
5. _____
6. _____
7. _____
8. _____
9. _____
10. _____

2 LISTEN

Complete the word with the letters 'au', 'aw', 'ou', or 'ow'.

1. h____k
2. fr____d
3. ____thor
4. borr____
5. dr____
6. t____er
7. ____gust
8. ____nt
9. cr____n
10. br____n
11. s____nd
12. elb____
13. cl____n
14. arr____
15. S____th
16. r____nd
17. fl____er
18. foll____
19. narr____
20. acc____nt
21. comp____nd
22. ____thentic
23. ____ditory
24. f____ntain
25. ____esome
26. br____nie
27. ar____nd
28. am____nt
29. ____ction
30. ass____lt

3 COMMON WORDS LIST 10

Listen and repeat the words and sentences.

country	answer	story	food	sun
together	cross	hard	never	door
night	city	tree	letter	group
children	example	always	mountain	real

1. What country is this?
2. This city is so big!
3. Do not cross the street now!
4. I always answer your calls.
5. There is a tall tree in the mountain.
6. The children like to read books.
7. We better cross the street together.
8. She is a good example in her class.
9. I got a letter last night.
10. I always pray in the mornings.
11. It is hard to get a job.
12. I like my group of friends.
13. I don't know the answer to that.
14. Children are nice.
15. She always sends me letters.

4 Label the pictures.

_____ _____

_____ _____

_____ _____

Homework: Practice reading words and sentences.

Lesson 50

1 word search
Find the 16 words hidden.
Write the words on the lines provided.

```
c c y d o w n p x e n a f d
l o x a l o u d t o w e r r
o u t l t a u c t i o n o a
u n l l s h a w k t v l w w
d t c o w x c s t e d n n d
f u f w a s t r o n a u t k
s g r o w q a s s a u l t o
a p p l a u d x b o s r o w
```

At Home

1 _____
2 _____
3 _____
4 _____
5 _____
6 _____
7 _____
8 _____
9 _____
10 _____
11 _____
12 _____
13 _____
14 _____
15 _____
16 _____

2 Label the pictures.

_____   _____   _____

_____   _____   _____

_____   _____   _____

_____   _____   _____

_____   _____   _____

_____   _____   _____

3 Write the words you learned with each special sound.

AU
1. _____ 7. _____
2. _____ 8. _____
3. _____ 9. _____
4. _____ 10. _____
5. _____ 11. _____
6. _____ 12. _____

AW
1. _____ 5. _____
2. _____ 6. _____
3. _____ 7. _____
4. _____ 8. _____

OU
1. _____ 11. _____
2. _____ 12. _____
3. _____ 13. _____
4. _____ 14. _____
5. _____ 15. _____
6. _____ 16. _____
7. _____ 17. _____
8. _____ 18. _____
9. _____ 19. _____
10. _____ 20. _____

OW
1. _____ 11. _____
2. _____ 12. _____
3. _____ 13. _____
4. _____ 14. _____
5. _____ 15. _____
6. _____ 16. _____
7. _____ 17. _____
8. _____ 18. _____
9. _____ 19. _____
10. _____ 20. _____

UNIT 5

INTRODUCTION

In this unit, you will learn words with 'oi/oy', and 'oo' sounds and words spelled with 'Y'.

Later, you will practice reading 'two-syllable' words and multi-syllable words, and work with root words, prefixes, and suffixes as well as words with special vowel combinations and special sounds or endings.

Finally, you will continue to practice reading and writing sentences as well as reading Bible scriptures.

OBJECTIVES

- Identify words with 'oi/oy' sounds.
- Use words with 'oo' sounds.
- Learn words with 'Y'.
- Learn 'two-syllable words'.
- Learn about root words, prefixes and suffixes.
- Use words with special vowel combinations and word endings 'tion/sion'.
- Practice reading multi-syllable words.

Lesson 51

🎧 51.1 WORDS WITH 'OI / OY'

These combinations have the sound of 'oi'. The letter 'Y' is a vowel.

OI

| BOIL | COIN | POINT | SOIL | OIL | AVOID | JOIN | ANOINT |
| BROIL | CHOICE | SPOIL | TOILET | VOICE | NOISE | NOISY | JOINT |

OY

| ROY | DESTROY | BOY | ANNOY | CONVOY | JOY | COWBOY | TOY |

When you hear the 'oi' sound at the end of a word, it is 'OY'. The vowels 'OI' never end a word.

🎧 51.2 WORDS WITH 'OO'

These two vowel combinations have two slightly different sounds.

ōō (long 'O' sound)

| TOO | POOL | ZOO | SCHOOL | MOON | BALLOON | SHOOT |
| TOOL | GOOSE | SOON | STOOL | BOOT | BAMBOO | SPOON |

ŏŏ (short 'U' sound)

| LOOK | BOOK | FOOT | WOOD | *BROOM | POOR | *ROOM |
| COOK | HOOD | TOOK | WOODEN | COOKIE | SHOOK | WOOL |

Words that have an asterisk (*) are usually pronounced in both ways.

Homework: Practice writing the words.

1 🎧 51.3 READING PRACTICE

Listen and repeat the sentences.

1. The wáter boiled after 20 minutes.
2. Please put more soil on the plant.
3. The toy car belongs to the boy.
4. Let's swim at the pool after school!
5. Who took the white stool?
6. I need a good tool to fix the sink soon.
7. Do your children like the zoo?
8. My grandma bakes good cookies.
9. Do you like cowboy movies?
10. Look! The moon is so big!
11. He reads a book about a big goose.
12. Can you cook?
13. Those boots look good on you!

Homework: Practice reading the sentences.

Dictation

1. _____ 13. _____
2. _____ 14. _____
3. _____ 15. _____
4. _____ 16. _____
5. _____ 17. _____
6. _____ 18. _____
7. _____ 19. _____
8. _____ 20. _____
9. _____ 21. _____
10. _____ 22. _____
11. _____ 23. _____
12. _____ 24. _____

Lesson 52

At Home

1 Unscramble
Unscramble the words.
Write the answers on the lines.

1. nomo _____
2. iolb _____
3. inoc _____
4. lopo _____
5. noso _____
6. iospl _____
7. oklo _____
8. kobo _____
9. jyo _____
10. njio _____
11. ofot _____
12. loto _____
13. ropo _____
14. mroo _____
15. yto _____
16. ivoec _____
17. ilos _____
18. nonay _____
19. oodw _____
20. otsoh _____

2 WRITING
Write the words for each sound.

OY
1. _____
2. _____
3. _____
4. _____
5. _____
6. _____
7. _____
8. _____

OI
1. _____
2. _____
3. _____
4. _____
5. _____
6. _____
7. _____
8. _____
9. _____
10. _____
11. _____
12. _____

OO
1. _____
2. _____
3. _____
4. _____
5. _____
6. _____
7. _____
8. _____
9. _____
10. _____
11. _____
12. _____

3 Label the pictures.

_____ _____ _____ _____ _____

_____ _____ _____ _____ _____

_____ _____ _____ _____ _____

4 WRITING
Write sentences with the words from above.

1.- _____
2.- _____
3.- _____
4.- _____
5.- _____

Lesson 53

At Home

1 Complete the message using the words from the box.

> Matthew 5: 9-10
>
> Great _____ belong to those who _____ to bring _____. _____ will _____ them his _____ and _____.
>
> Great blessings _____ to those who suffer _____ for doing what is _____. God's _____ belongs to them.

| belong | persecution | blessings | sons | kingdom | right |
| work | | daughters | peace | God | call |

2 Label the pictures.

_____   _____   _____   _____   _____

_____   _____   _____   _____   _____

3 WRITING
Write sentences with the words from above.

1.- _____
2.- _____
3.- _____
4.- _____
5.- _____
6.- _____
7.- _____

Lesson 54

LETTER Y

1 'Y' AS A CONSONANT

Letter 'Y' is a consonant when it starts a word.

YO-YO	YES	YOU	YARD	YEAR
YOGURT	YELL	YARN	YAK	YOUR
YELLOW	YOLK	YATCH	YAM	YOGA

2 'Y' AS A VOWEL

Letter 'Y' is considered a vowel when the word has only one syllable and letter 'Y' is the only vowel in the word. It sounds 'i'.

MYTH   RHYTHM

3 'Y' WITH 'AI' SOUND

Letter 'Y' has a long sound 'ai' when it ends a one syllable word. It sounds 'ai' also when the vowel 'Y' stands alone.

CRY	MY	BY	TRY	FLY	FRY
SKY	WHY	SHY	SPY	DRY	

4 'Y' AS IN CRYPT

Letter 'Y' sounds 'i' when it is followed by one or two consonants.

Dictation

1. _____
2. _____
3. _____
4. _____
5. _____
6. _____
7. _____
8. _____
9. _____
10. _____
11. _____
12. _____
13. _____
14. _____
15. _____
16. _____
17. _____
18. _____
19. _____
20. _____

Homework: **Practice writing the words.**

Matthew 5:13-16

"You are the salt of the earth. But if the salt loses its taste, it cannot be made salty again. Salt is useless if it loses its salty taste. It will be thrown out where people will just walk on it."

"You are the light that shines for the world to see. You are like a city built on a hill that cannot be hidden. People don't hide a lamp under a bowl. They put it on a lampstand. Then the light shines for everyone in the house. In the same way, you should be a light for other people. Live so that they will see the good things you do and praise your Father in heaven."

5 WRITE
Write sentences with the words from above.

1.-_____
2.-_____
3.-_____
4.-_____
5.-_____

Lesson 55

At Home

WORDS WITH 'Y'

1 Complete the sentences using words with 'Y'.

1.- I like to eat the _____ of the egg.
2.- That is _____ _____ hat.
3.- Please do not _____. I am here.
4.- I want to see the _____ at the zoo.
5.- This will be a great _____ for me.
6.- Is this _____ _____? Mine is cold.

YOGURT   YAK   YEAR   YELLOW   YOUR   MY   YELL   YOLK

3 WORDS WITH Y
Write the words with letter 'Y'.

1 _____   10 _____
2 _____   11 _____
3 _____   12 _____
4 _____   13 _____
5 _____   14 _____
6 _____   15 _____
7 _____   16 _____
8 _____   17 _____
9 _____   18 _____

2 Label the pictures.

4 Unscramble
Unscramble the words.
Write the correct words on the lines.

1. yhw   _____
2. rcy   _____
3. arye   _____
4. uyor   _____
5. kay   _____
6. rdya   _____
7. agyo   _____
8. rnay   _____
9. tycah   _____
10. kloy   _____
11. rfy   _____
12. dyr   _____
13. lyf   _____
14. roygtu _____
15. leyl   _____
16. llyeow _____

Matthew 5:13-16

Write T(True) or F(False) on the line.

_____1.- Jesus wants us to be the salt of the earth.
_____2.- We can not use salt if it loses its taste.
_____3.- Jesus compares us to a city built on a hill.
_____4.- A city built on a hill can be hidden.
_____5.- People don't hide a lamp under a bowl.
_____6.- I should be a light for other people.
_____7.- I should be a good example to others.

MORE WORDS WITH 'Y' 🎧 56.1

1 'Y' IN SILENT 'E' SKILL   TYPE

When a one syllable word ends with 'E', the 'E' is silent and the first vowel in the word is long.

STYLE   TYPE

2 A VOWEL + 'Y'   MAY

When there are vowels together in a one syllable word, the first vowel is long and the second vowel is silent.

MAY	DAY	SAY	BAY	GRAY	SPRAY
PLAY	KEY	PAY	STAY	PRAY	STRAY

3 'Y' IN A 2 SYLLABLE WORD   LAZY

It sounds 'i' at the end of a 2 syllable word when there is a vowel in the first syllable. The 'Y' sounds 'i' and the first vowel in the word has a long sound.

LAZY	LADY	EASY	BABY	COZY
TONY	TINY	SHINY	CRAZY	NAVY

4 'Y' AFTER DOUBLE CONSONANTS   HAPPY

'Y' sounds 'i' at the end of a 2 syllable word when there is a vowel in the first syllable of the word, followed by double consonants. The vowel has a short sound.

FUNNY	DIZZY	SILLY	HAPPY	PIGGY
LIZZY	MERRY	TEDDY	BILLY	DADDY

5 WRITE
Write sentences with words that have the sounds of 'Y'.

1.-_____
2.-_____
3.-_____
4.-_____
5.-_____

Dictation

1._____
2._____
3._____
4._____
5._____
6._____
7._____
8._____
9._____
10._____
11._____
12._____
13._____
14._____
15._____
16._____
17._____
18._____
19._____
20._____

Homework: Practice writing the words.

Lesson 56

At Home

Lesson 57

MORE WORDS WITH 'Y'

1 Write words that have the sounds of 'Y'.

1._____	11._____
2._____	12._____
3._____	13._____
4._____	14._____
5._____	15._____
6._____	16._____
7._____	17._____
8._____	18._____
9._____	19._____
10._____	20._____

2 **Unscramble**
Unscramble the words in the box.
Write the correct words on the lines provided.

1.- lisly _____	11.- ysrpa _____
2.- ryrem _____	12.- tarsy _____
3.- yfnun _____	13.- itny _____
4.- izydz _____	14.- nisyh _____
5.- ybab _____	15.- lpay _____
6.- seay _____	16.- dyadd _____
7.- zoyc _____	17.- yaphp _____
8.- vnay _____	18.- giypg _____
9.- ylaz _____	19.- yek _____
10.- dyal _____	20.- rycaz _____

Homework: Practice writing the words.

3 Label the pictures.

_____ _____ _____ _____ _____

_____ _____ _____ _____ _____

4 **The Bible**

NEW TESTAMENT

Matthew	John
Mark	Acts
Luke	Romans

Answer:

1. Which of these books have you read?

2. Which books are letters by Paul?

3. Which books relate the life of Christ?

MATTHEW
A brief history of the life of Christ.

MARK
A brief history of the life of Christ.

LUKE
The history of the life of Christ, it refers to his most important acts and discourses.

JOHN
The life of Christ, with important discourses.

ACTS
The history of the acts of the apostles and of the foundation of the Christian Church.

ROMANS
A letter by Paul to the Romans.

Lesson 58

TWO SYLLABLE WORDS

1 🎧 58.1 The first syllable ends with a long vowel sound. If there is one consonant after the first vowel, it goes in the second syllable. The first vowel has a long sound since it stands alone in the syllable.

MŪ·SĬC   PĪ·LŎT   Ō·PĔN   RĀ·ZŎR   RŌ·BŎT   RĪ·VAL

Practice reading the following two-syllable words:

BA·CON	SI·LENT	RO·DENT	HO·TEL	RE·CESS	PU·PIL	RA·DAR
VI·RUS	BA·SIC	CE·MENT	FE·VER	MO·TEL	NA·TION	HE·RO
DI·GEST	SE·CRET	LE·GAL	I·TEM	SI·REN	MA·JOR	LA·BEL
E·VEN	VA·POR	FLA·VOR	MO·MENT	CLO·VER	FI·BER	HU·MAN

Notice that words follow the pattern : **V·CV**   (vowel • Consonant • Vowel)

2 🎧 58.2 If there is a letter 'E' at the end of the word, you must apply the silent 'E' rule.

CĀ·BLE   TĀ·BLE   RŌ·TĀTE   Ū·NĪTE

Practice reading the following multi-syllable words:

| SI·LENCE | CA·BLE | U·NITE | BE·HAVE | RE·VISE | PO·LITE | DO·NATE |
| CLI·MATE | DE·LETE | RO·TATE | PRO·VIDE | RI·FLE | STA·PLE | LO·CATE |

Homework: Practice writing the words.
Use the words in sentences.

Dictation

1. _____   11. _____
2. _____   12. _____
3. _____   13. _____
4. _____   14. _____
5. _____   15. _____
6. _____   16. _____
7. _____   17. _____
8. _____   18. _____
9. _____   19. _____
10. _____ 20. _____

4 🎧 58.3 **READING PRACTICE**
Listen and repeat the sentences.

1. I like to eat bacon and eggs in the morning.
2. The children like to play soccer in recess time.
3. I heard the sound of a siren.
4. They will stay in a nice hotel during vacations.
5. I saw the price of the cap on the label.
6. I will invite my friend to the church.
7. I need to delete some files from my laptop.
8. There is a good climate in this country.
9. Please keep silence in the library.
10. The pupils behave very well at school.
11. My brother is a pilot.
12. I like to listen to country music.

Homework: Practice reading the sentences.

Lesson 59

At Home

TWO SYLLABLE WORDS

1 Label the pictures.

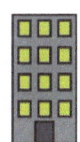    

_____ _____ _____ _____ _____

_____ _____ _____ _____ _____

_____ _____ _____ _____ _____

   LEMON GRAPE

_____ _____ _____ _____ _____

2 WRITING
Write sentences with the words from above.

1. _____
2. _____
3. _____
4. _____

3 MATCH
Find the right word from the box.

| delete   rotate   hotel   secret   cement |
| fever   silence |

1. _____ the Earth does this around the sun..
2. _____ a place to stay when you are traveling.
3. _____ this is used in constructions.
4. _____ when your body temperature is high.
5. _____ something you can not tell others.
6. _____ this is another word for erase.
7. _____ this is the opposite of noise.

4 word search
Find the 18 words hidden.
Write the words on the lines provided.

```
t m r o b o t o t b i v v
a u i d i g e s t a t i d
s s v f e v e r r c e r o
e i a l a b e l v o m u n
c c l g l c e m e n t s a
r a z o r b i b a s i c t
e p i l o t o m a j o r e
t a b l e e r o d e n t t
```

_____   _____
_____   _____
_____   _____
_____   _____
_____   _____
_____   _____
_____   _____
_____   _____
_____   _____

Lesson 60

TWO SYLLABLE WORDS II

1. You must identify the R-Controlled vowels 'AR, ER, IR, OR, UR'.
They do not separate. They keep their special sound.

TI·GER   SPI·DER   PA·PER   CLO·VER

FOR·SAKE   TUR·KEY   TUR·TLE   SHER·IFF   CLEV·ER   LIZ·ARD

2. If the vowel is followed by two consonants, divide between them. The first vowel in the word has a short sound.

OB·JECT   PIC·TURE   LOB·STER   PEN·CIL   PLAS·TIC

COR·NER   AR·THUR   OR·PHAN   GAR·DEN   CIR·CLE

Notice that most of these words follow the pattern : **VC·CV** (Vowel , Consonant · Consonant , Vowel)

SIG·NAL	SIS·TER	DOC·TOR	EL·BOW	CUS·TOM	EN·JOY	TAR·GET
GEN·TLE	EN·JOY	HAM·STER	CON·TEST	PIS·TOL	PLEN·TY	CAS·TLE
PUR·PLE	CAN·DY	COM·PETE	BAP·TIZE	PROB·LEM	FOR·BID	WIN·DOW
SUB·JECT	FAN·CY	WON·DER	BAS·KET	COM·PLETE	EX·CUSE	COM·BINE

Homework: Practice writing the words.
Use the words in sentences.

Dictation

1. _____   11. _____
2. _____   12. _____
3. _____   13. _____
4. _____   14. _____
5. _____   15. _____
6. _____   16. _____
7. _____   17. _____
8. _____   18. _____
9. _____   19. _____
10. _____ 20. _____

New Testament

| I Corinthians | Galatians | Philippians |
| II Corinthians | Ephesians | Colossians |

I CORINTHIANS
A letter from Paul to the Corinthians, referring to some needs of the church.

II CORINTHIANS
Paul confirms his disciples in their faith.

GALATIANS
Explains that we are justified by faith and not by work.

EPHESIANS
Paul explains the new identity believers have in Christ.

PHILIPPIANS
Paul talks about Christian behavior.

COLOSSIANS
Paul warns his disciples against errors.

At Home

Lesson 61

TWO SYLLABLE WORDS II

1 Label the pictures.

_____ _____ _____ _____ _____

_____ _____ _____ _____ _____

_____ _____ _____ _____ _____

_____ _____ _____ _____ _____

2 Complete

LETTER	PAUL	CORINTHIANS	CHURCH
ERRORS	ACTS	CHRISTIAN	IDENTITY

I CORINTHIANS
A_____ from Paul to the _____, referring to some needs of the _____.

GALATIANS
Explains that we are justified by faith and not by_____.

PHILIPPIANS
Paul talks about _____ behavior.

COLOSSIANS
Paul warns his disciples against _____.

3 word search
Find the 15 words hidden.
Write the words on the lines provided.

```
t u r k e y f c c e h c
a e b h p r o b l e m u
r w o n d e r a e m c s
g c a n d y s s v y a t
e o n g e q a k e z s o
t u r t l e k e r t t m
s p u r p l e t u k l p
m t w i n d o w t a e o
```

_____
_____
_____
_____
_____
_____
_____
_____
_____
_____
_____
_____
_____
_____
_____

66

Lesson 62

1  If the vowel is followed by double consonants, the vowel has a short sound. Divide the word between the two consonants.

CŎM·MON   ĂP·PLE   BĂL·LOON   PĔN·NY   SŎC·CER   SCĬS·SORS

Notice that words follow the pattern: **VC·CV**   (Vowel Consonant • Consonant Vowel)

Practice reading the following words. Mark the special sounds.

COM·MAND	LET·TUCE	AR·ROW	DIZ·ZY	RIB·BON	CAT·TLE
FOL·LOW	SUM·MER	COT·TON	PUP·PY	HAP·PEN	FUN·NY
CUR·RENT	BOT·TLE	BUN·NY	HUR·RY	TRAF·FIC	COL·LECT
CHANNEL	DINNER	HAPPEN	COFFEE	MESSY	SILLY

2 If the vowel is followed by one consonant, divide after it. The first syllable will have a short sound since the vowel has one or two consonants.

CĬT·Y   CRĬT·IC   FŎR·EST   LĬM·IT   ĬM·AGE   HŎN·EY

Notice that words follow the pattern: **VC·V**   (Vowel • Consonant, Vowel)

Practice reading the following words. Mark the special sounds.

PRES·ENT	HAB·IT	HON·OR	CAB·IN	CAM·EL	CRED·IT
DRAG·ON	FOR·EST	FIN·ISH	LEV·EL	LEM·ON	NICK·EL
MON·EY	CIV·IL	CHAP·EL	STUD·Y	MED·AL	MEN·U

Homework: Practice reading the words.

Dictation

1. _____ 14. _____
2. _____ 15. _____
3. _____ 16. _____
4. _____ 17. _____
5. _____ 18. _____
6. _____ 19. _____
7. _____ 20. _____
8. _____ 21. _____
9. _____ 22. _____
10. _____ 23. _____
11. _____ 24. _____
12. _____ 25. _____
13. _____ 26. _____

4 Books of The New Testament

| I Thessalonians | I Timothy | Titus |
| II Thessalonians | II Timothy | Philemon |

I THESSALONIANS
Paul exhorts the disciples to continue in the faith.

II THESSALONIANS
Paul corrects some errors concerning the second coming of Christ.

I AND II TIMOTHY
Paul instructs Timothy in his duties, and encourages him in the work of the ministry.

TITUS
Paul encourages Titus in the performance of his ministerial duties.

PHILEMON
A letter from Paul to Philemon to express the changes of a believer.

Lesson 63

At Home

TWO SYLLABLE WORDS III

1 Label the pictures.

2 WRITING
Write sentences with the words from above.

1.- _____
2.- _____
3.- _____

3 WORD SEARCH
Find the 13 words hidden.
Write the words on the lines provided.

```
p r e s e n t c d r a g o n
e e b u p r o r i s b o l i
n c o m m a n d z a u c o c
n c a m d y s s z k n o c k
y o n e s t u d y y n m l e
t c c r e n i t r o y m e l
a s u t e l e t h o n o r p
p u p p y c a b i n s n d j
```

1. _____
2. _____
3. _____
4. _____
5. _____
6. _____
7. _____
8. _____
9. _____
10. _____
11. _____
12. _____
13. _____

4 UNSCRAMBLE
Unscramble the words.
Write the correct word on the line.

1. rceosc _____
2. sorsiscs _____
3. tletceu _____
4. ollwof _____
5. nrucret _____
6. ltboet _____
7. ybnnu _____
8. toncto _____
9. yurrh _____
10. epnhap _____
11. tclate _____
13. nfynu _____
13. tcirci _____
14. sertof _____

68

UNIT 6

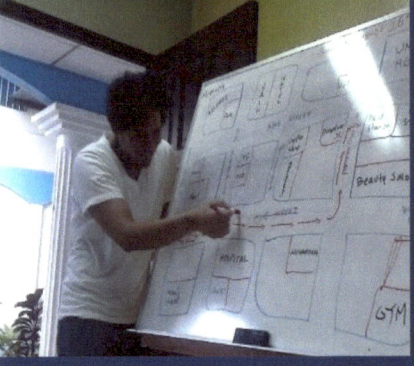

INTRODUCTION

In this unit, you will learn words with 'oi/oy', and 'oo' sounds. We aim students to use words spelled with 'Y'. As well as practice reading 'two-syllable' words.

You will work with root words, prefixes, and suffixes as well as words with special vowel combinations and special sounds or endings.

You will also learn some multi-syllable words.

Finally, you will continue to practice reading and writing sentences as well as reading Bible scriptures.

OBJECTIVES

- Practice adding prefixes, and suffixes to form new words.
- Identify root words.
- Learn some word endings and how to add them to words correctly.
- Read special vowel combinations correctly.

Lesson 64

PREFIXES

PREFIXES: are combinations of letters added at the beginning of root words to change their meanings.

ROOT WORD: stands on its own as a word but you can use it to make new words from it by adding a prefix or a suffix.

1 RE indicates repetition. It means 'again'. It also means 'back', or backward meaning.   RĔ·FĬLL   RĒ·DO

REBUILD   REDO   REREAD   REFOLD   REGAIN   RETURN
REDYE   REWRITE   RESELL   REMIND   REFLECT

2 BE indicates to surround completely, to affect completely or to consider as cause to be   BĒ·SĪDE

BEHAVIOR   BELIEVE   BECOME   BESIDE   BEHOLD

3 MIS means incorrect, wrong, a lack of.   MĬS·SPELL

MISPRONOUNCE   MISBELIEVE   MISSPELL   MISREAD   MISCALCULATE   MISJUDGE

4 DIS most of the time it indicates opposite or absence of   DĪS·CŌVER

DISCOVER   DISADVANTAGE   DISAGREE   DISAPPEAR   DISORDER   DISAPPOINT
DISCUSSION   DISCOUNT   DISINFECTANT   DISGUSTED   DISHONEST   DISOBEY

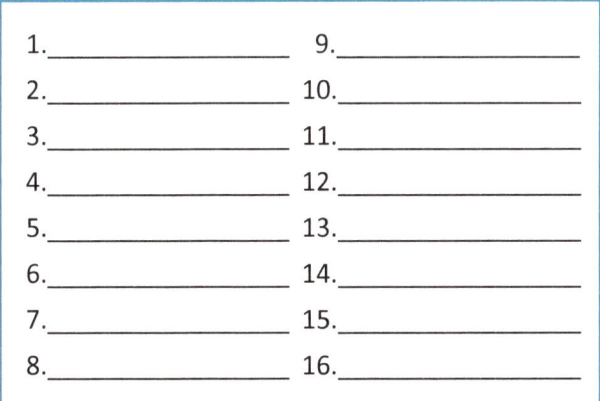

Dictation

1._____ 9._____
2._____ 10._____
3._____ 11._____
4._____ 12._____
5._____ 13._____
6._____ 14._____
7._____ 15._____
8._____ 16._____

6 READING PRACTICE

Listen and practice reading the sentences.

1. I must redo the lesson for tomorrow.
2. My best friend likes to discover new things.
3. I am sorry but I disagree with you.
4. I misspelled the word in the dictation.
5. I want to become a doctor in the future.
6. We believe in God.
7. That book has a good discount.
8. Please rewrite the sentences.

Homework: Practice reading the sentences.

7 Write the words that can be added each of the prefixes.

RE	**DIS**	**BE**	**MIS**
1._____	1._____	1._____	1._____
2._____	2._____	2._____	2._____
3._____	3._____	3._____	3._____
4._____	4._____	4._____	4._____

Lesson 65

1 MATCH
Add the prefix 're' or 'be' to each word to form a new word.

1. _____ build
2. _____ havior
3. _____ come
4. _____ loved
5. _____ do
6. _____ read
7. _____ write
8. _____ hold
9. _____ friend
10. ____ dye
11. _____ turn
12. _____ arrange
13. _____ iterate
14. _____ side
15. _____ sell
16. _____ mind
17. _____ flect
18. _____ lieve
19. _____ fold
20. _____ tell

2 MATCH
Add the prefix 'mis' or 'dis' to each word to form a new word.

1. _____ obey
2. _____ courage
3. _____ charge
4. _____ believe
5. _____ spell
6. _____ order
7. _____ color
8. _____ read
9. _____ inform
10. _____ continue
11. _____ cussion
12. _____ comfort
13. _____ agree
14. _____ judge
15. _____ trust
16. _____ calculate
17. _____ gusted
18. _____ appoint
19. _____ armed
20. _____ believe

3 WRITE THE WORD
Write the word that means the opposite or incorrect on the line provided.

1. abilities _____
2. approve _____
3. continue _____
4. advantage _____
5. courage _____
6. armed _____
7. comfort _____
8. connect _____
9. spell _____
10. inform _____
11. believe _____
12. read _____
13. obey _____
14. judge _____
15. pronounce _____

4 WRITING
Write sentences with the words from exercise 2.

1. _____
2. _____
3. _____
4. _____
5. _____

5 WORD SEARCH
Find the 12 words hidden.
Write the words on the lines provided.

```
m i s r e p r e s e n t o e r
i e b e h o l d r e g a i n o
s d i s c o u r a g e d r r s
t c a u d m i s r e a d e e e
r o n r e i t e r a t e f t p
u c c d i s c o l o r t o u l
s s u t e d e t h o n t l r r
t d i s c o v e r n s b d n n
```

1. _____
2. _____
3. _____
4. _____
5. _____
6. _____
7. _____
8. _____
9. _____
10. _____
11. _____
12. _____

6 UNSCRAMBLE
Unscramble the words.
Write the answer on the line.

1. icdftsomor _____
2. dosicaureg _____
3. ydere _____
4. tiwerer _____
5. elvbiee _____
6. robheavi _____
7. sbedie _____
8. graeni _____
9. donisetcnt _____
10. ddroiser _____
11. lodcisro _____
13. bdoiesy _____
13. imseplsl _____
14. mirinofms _____

71

Lesson 66

SUFFIXES, AND ROOT WORDS

SUFFIXES: are combinations of letters added at the end of the root words.
ROOT WORD: is the base word from which other words are derived by adding a suffix.

1. ER — 'ER' is added to the verb to show a person who does that action — PLAY·ER

PLAYER	EMPLOYER	TEACHER	PAINTER	DRIVER	PUNISHER	EXPLORER
DANCER	FOREIGNER	PITCHER	BELIEVER	WRITER	WINNER	SPEAKER
HUNTER	BANKER	FARMER	WORKER	LEADER	BUTCHER	CATCHER

2. LESS means without — HOPE·LESS

ENDLESS	FEARLESS	CARELESS	HOPELESS	USELESS	RESTLESS	HOMELESS

3. FUL means full — HARM·FUL

BEAUTIFUL	DOUBTFUL	CAREFUL	GRATEFUL	WONDERFUL	COLORFUL	PAINFUL
GRACEFUL	PEACEFUL	HARMFUL	SUCCESSFUL	POWERFUL	THANKFUL	CHEERFUL

4. OR indicates a person who does that action — DOCT·OR

ACTOR	COLLECTOR	SUPERVISOR	AUTHOR	NARRATOR	ANCESTOR	DOCTOR
DONOR	DICTATOR	TRANSLATOR	SAILOR	SENATOR	TAILOR	MENTOR

Dictation

1. _____ 11. _____
2. _____ 12. _____
3. _____ 13. _____
4. _____ 14. _____
5. _____ 15. _____
6. _____ 16. _____
7. _____ 17. _____
8. _____ 18. _____
9. _____ 19. _____
10. _____ 20. _____

6. READING PRACTICE

Listen and practice reading the sentences.

1. He is a famous actor in my country.
2. I need to call the tailor tomorrow.
3. These jeans are useless. They are too old.
4. The farmer has a new tractor in his farm.
5. I do not feel so good. I need to see a doctor.
6. Let's pray for homeless people every day.
7. I am thankful for my teacher.
8. Please don't be careless with your work.
9. My father is a hard worker.
10. My sister is a beautiful girl. She's wonderful.

Homework: Practice reading the sentences.

Lesson 67

1 MATCH
Add the suffix 'er' or 'less' to form new words.

1. play _____
2. bank _____
3. driv _____
4. hope _____
5. catch _____

6. paint _____
7. fear _____
8. work _____
9. lead _____
10. hunt _____

11. end _____
12. butch _____
13. speak _____
14. rest _____
15. care _____

16. danc _____
17. employ _____
18. winn _____
19. explor _____
20. believ _____

2 MATCH
Add the prefix 'ful' or 'or' to form new words.

1. act _____
2. don _____
3. sail _____
4. auth _____
5. doct _____

6. color _____
7. ment _____
8. collect _____
9. grate _____
10. cheer _____

11. peace _____
12. grace _____
13. care _____
14. pain _____
15. thank _____

16. ancest _____
17. senat _____
18. dictat _____
19. power _____
20. wonder _____

3 WRITING
Write sentences with the words with suffixes.

1. _____
2. _____
3. _____
4. _____
5. _____

4 Circle the suffix in each word.
Then write the suffix on the line provided.

1. successful _____
2. powerful _____
3. homeless _____
4. harmful _____
5. doctor _____
6. explorer _____
7. thankful _____
8. wonderful _____
9. supervisor _____
10. ancestor _____
11. colorful _____
12. careful _____
13. grateful _____
14. restless _____
15. hopeless _____

5 WORD SEARCH
Find the 10 words hidden.
Write the words on the lines provided.

```
c i s t a i l o r e u o g c
a u t h o r l d r e s i n o
r d u s c d o n o r e r d l
e c a u d m i s r e l e o o
l o n r a c t o r a e f d r
e c c d i s c o l o s i t f
s e n a t o r t h o s s o u
s d i h o m e l e s s d r l
```

1. _____
2. _____
3. _____
4. _____
5. _____
6. _____
7. _____
8. _____
9. _____
10. _____

6 UNSCRAMBLE
Unscramble the words.
Write the answer on the line.

1. fdutobl _____
2. lucfrae _____
3. clpeaeuf _____
4. lcfrageu _____
5. lufitbae _____
6. rotnraar _____
7. stancreo _____
8. orsvurpei _____
9. rlatsntaro _____
10. rotcoelcl _____
11. tmenor _____
13. lfhraum _____
14. slfuccseu _____
15. lhftunak _____
16. eraclfu _____

73

Lesson 68

WORD ENDINGS

1. 'TION' sounds 'shun'

The letters 'TION' always stay together and are always located at the end of the words.
When there is a vowel 'I' before 'TION', this has a short sound.

CŎN·DĬ·TION   DĚ·SCRĬP·TION   STĀ·TION

| CONTRACTION | PRESCRIPTION | LOCATION | RETENTION | SITUATION |
| DISTRACTION | CONTRADICTION | VIOLATION | REPUTATION | VACATION |

2. 'SION' sounds 'shun'

MĬS·SION   DĬS·CŬS·SION   TĚL·Ě·VĬ·SION   EX·TĚN·SION

| EXPRESSION | EXPLOSION | TELEVISION | CONVERSION | EXPANSION |
| IMPRESSION | EXPULSION | DISCUSSION | PERMISSION | DIMENSION |

3. MULTI-SYLLABLE WORDS

Listen to the words. Practice reading the words.

EMERGENCY	DECEMBER	UNDERSTAND	DESTRUCTION	TECHNOLOGY
SUPERFICIAL	PHARMACY	CONFERENCE	PERSONALITY	PUNISHMENT
MEDICATION	SUPERSONIC	DISAGREEMENT	PRESENTATION	PUBLICATION

Homework: Practice writing the words.

Dictation

1. _____ 10. _____
2. _____ 11. _____
3. _____ 12. _____
4. _____ 13. _____
5. _____ 14. _____
6. _____ 15. _____
7. _____ 16. _____
8. _____ 17. _____
9. _____ 18. _____

| HEBREWS | I PETER | I JOHN |
| JAMES | II PETER | II JOHN |

HEBREWS
Teaches about Jesus.

JAMES
Talks about different aspects of our new life in Christ.

I AND II PETER
Exhorts Christians to live according to their new life in Christ.

I JOHN
Talks about the love of God to us and how we must reflect God's love by our good behavior.

II JOHN
Exhorts Christians to love others and warns them against false teachers.

Lesson 69

At Home

1 Label the pictures.

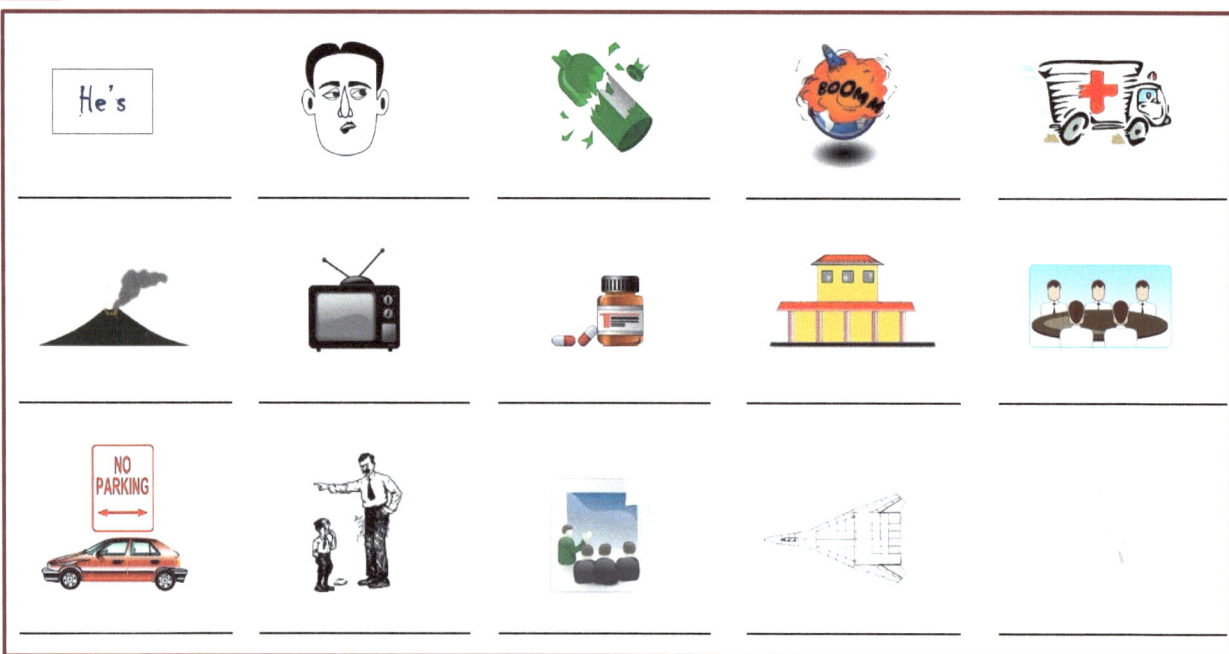

He's _____

2 Complete the sentences with the words from the box.

| distraction | permission | superficial | conference |
| personality | impression | disagreement | pharmacy |

1.- It is so important to leave a good _____ at a job interview.
2.- We have a very special _____ every year in the month of June.
3.- I need to get a _____ in my job for next week.
4.- My children used a good _____ to play in the park for another while.
5.- We have to avoid being _____ people.
6.- My friend needs to buy a medication at the _____.
7.- My baby daughter already shows her _____. She is so cute!
8.- The Bible says that we have to solve any kind of _____ among us.

3 SYLLABLES
Write the number of syllables in each word.

emergency ____   superficial ____   medication ____
December ____   pharmacy ____   destruction ____
understand ____   supersonic ____   disagreement ____
conference ____   personality ____   presentation ____
technology ____   punishment ____   publication ____

4 COMPLETE
Write the correct word ending.

vaca ____
distrac ____
loca ____
televi ____
discus ____
permis ____
expul ____
expres ____
exten ____
exposi ____
reten ____
contrac ____
contradic ____
explo ____
reputa ____
loca ____
viola ____
impres ____
dimen ____
expan ____

Lesson 70

1 SPECIAL VOWEL COMBINATIONS

When there are two vowels together, they will not be separated.
Remember adjacent vowels "OA, EE, EA, AI, OE, IE, UI."

FEAR·FUL   DREAM·ER   PAIN·LESS   HON·EY

DE·TAIL	COF·FEE	PEA·NUT	RE·PEAT	DE·CAY	MON·KEY
BLACK·OUT	BEA·VER	DE·GREE	FRI·DAY	SLEEP·Y	SUN·DAY
FOOL·ISH	FIF·TEEN	OB·TAIN	EX·PLAIN	TEA·POT	HON·EY

2 SPECIAL VOWEL SOUNDS

The vowel combinations 'AU, OU, OO' do not separate.

A·BOUT   COUN·TRY   FOOL·ISH   BE·CAUSE

AU·GUST	AUC·TION	BOOK·LET	COUNT·LESS	JOY·OUS	COUN·CIL
LOUD·ER	AUS·TERE	AU·THOR	AU·TUMN	BE·CAUSE	A·BOUT
A·LOUD	A·MOUNT	AN·XIOUS	AN·NOUNCE	A·ROUND	BLOW·OUT

Homework: Practice writing the words.

Dictation

1. _____
2. _____
3. _____
4. _____
5. _____
6. _____
7. _____
8. _____
9. _____
10. _____
11. _____
12. _____
13. _____
14. _____
15. _____
16. _____
17. _____
18. _____

III JOHN   JUDE   REVELATION

III JOHN
A letter to Gaius, praising him for his hospitality.

JUDE
Warnings against deceivers.

REVELATION
The future of the Church foretold.

5 UNSCRAMBLE

Unscramble the words.
Write the answer on the line.

1. towbulo   _____
2. sueabce   _____
3. muntua   _____
4. xoiasnu   _____
5. natmuo   _____
6. tblkoeo   _____

6 WORD SEARCH

Find the 10 words hidden.
Write the words on the lines provided.

```
c i s t o b t a i n u o p c
f o o l i s h f r e d i a o
p d d s a d o r o r r r i l
e c e u b m f i f t e e n o
a o g r o c t d r a a f l r
n c r d u s c a l o m o e f
u e e a t o r y h o e l s u
t d e f e a r f u l r d s l
```

1. _____
2. _____
3. _____
4. _____
5. _____
6. _____
7. _____
8. _____
9. _____
10. _____

At Home

Lesson 71

SPECIAL VOWEL COMBINATIONS & SPECIAL VOWEL SOUNDS

1 Label the pictures.

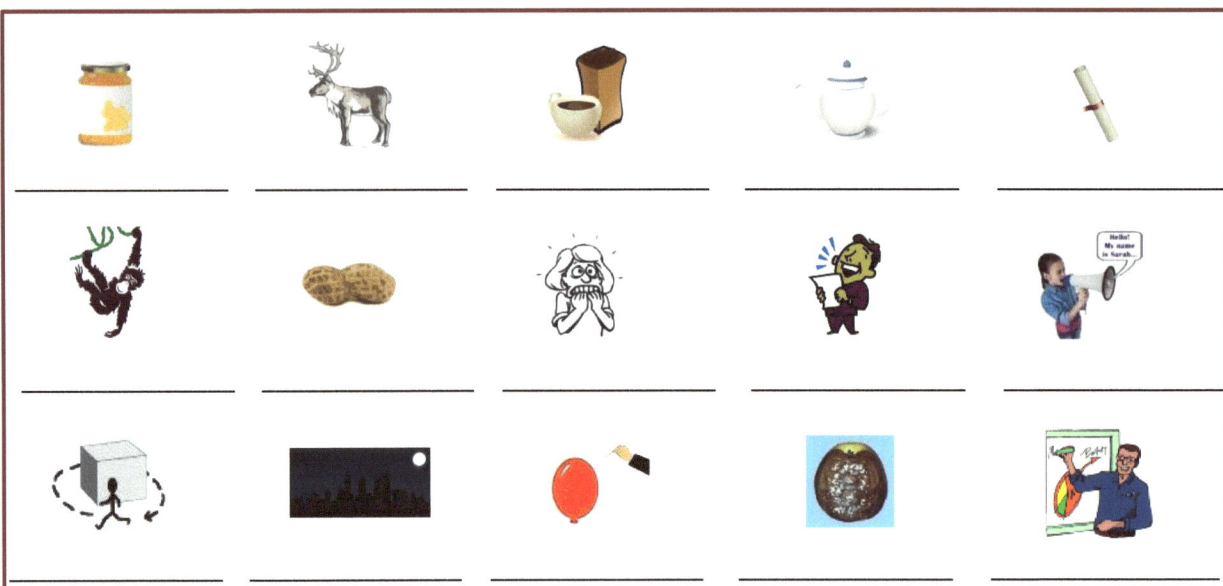

2 Match the words with their definition.

| fearful | dreamer | author |
| amount | decreases | repeat |

1. _____ to have fear.
2. _____ opposite of increase.
3. _____ a person full of dreams.
4. _____ to say things over and over again.
5. _____ the person who writes a book.
6. _____ the number of objects in a group.

4 COMPLETE
Write the missing letters.

1. p____ceful
2. f____lish
3. c____ncil
4. degr____
5. obt____n
6. ab____t
7. det____l
8. expl__n
9. blow____t
10. monk____
11. black____t
12. c____ntry
13. ___tumn
14. ar___nd
15. anx____s
16. al___d
17. ___gust
18. joy___s
19. b___klet
20. ___ction
21. hon___
22. p___nut
23. Frid___
24. bec___se
25. t___pot
26. Sund____

3 COMPLETE
Use the words from the box to complete the description of each book.

HEBREWS: Teaches about _____.
JAMES: Talks about different aspects of our new _____ in _____.
I AND II PETER: Exhort _____ to live according to their new life in Christ.
I JOHN: Talks about the _____ of _____ to us.
II JOHN: Exhorts Christians to love _____ and warms them against false _____.

GOD
CHRIST
JESUS
LOVE
LIFE
OTHERS
TEACHERS
CHRISTIANS

UNIT 7

ESOLCHILDREN - SAN PEDRO SULA

INTRODUCTION

In this unit, you will learn some common words and expressions for greeting people, as well as some formal and informal farewells and expressions to share personal information. You will learn the numbers from 1 to 1000.

Later, you will practice using personal pronouns and possessive adjectives. You will learn some titles used for people.

Finally, you will learn a Bible story related to meeting people and also some of the names given to God and Jesus.

OBJECTIVES

- Greet people.
- Share personal information and meet people.
- Say the numbers from 1 to 1000.
- Use personal pronouns correctly.
- Use possessive adjectives correctly.
- Learn some titles used when referring to people.
- Learn some names given to God and Jesus.

Lesson 72

Who is God?

Luke 1:47
I am very happy because God is my Savior.

Job 31:4
God is the one who knows what I do and sees every step I take.

Answer:
- Who is God for you?
- Is God your savior?
- What do you think about these Scriptures?

3 🎧 72.3 Meeting People
Listen to the dialogue. Then read it in pairs.

Danilo: Good morning, my name is Danilo. What's your name?
Oscar: Hi, my name is Oscar. Nice to meet you!
Danilo: Pleased to meet you Oscar.
Oscar: How are you today?
Danilo: I am fine, thank you.

Tim: Hello, my name's Tim. What's your name?
Beth: Hi, I'm Beth. It's nice to meet you! This is my friend Gina.
Tim: Hi. Pleased to meet you Gina.
Gina: Hi. It's nice to meet you too. How are you?
Tim: I'm fine. Thanks. How are you doing?
Beth: I'm doing well.

1 Greetings and farewells

Formal Greetings	Formal Farewells	Formal conversation
Hello!	Bye!	Thank you
Good morning	Good bye!	Thank you so much!
Good afternoon	See you later!	Yes
Good evening	See you tomorrow!	no
Good night	Good Night!	

Informal Greetings		Informal Farewells	Informal conversation
Hi!	Hey!	Bye!	Thanks!
Hello!	Hi there!	Take care!	Thanks a lot!
Morning!		See you!	Yeah!
			Nope!

'Good evening' is used when you meet someone in the evening.
'Good night' is used when you leave to go to bed.

4 Practice

a. Complete the conversations with the phrases in the box. Then listen and check.

My name is Peter	Good evening	What's your name?
Nice to meet you	I'm great!	See you later

Peter: _____. I'm Peter.
Peter: _____
Ted: _____. How are you doing?
Peter: _____. Pleased to meet you!
Ted: _____. See you soon.
Peter: _____.

b. Write the words in order to form common phrases used when meeting people.

1.- doing / are / how / you
_____

2.- later / you / see
_____

3.- tomorrow / you / see
_____

4.- meet / to / nice / you
_____

c. Work in pairs. Write a dialogue.
_____
_____
_____
_____
_____

Good morning!

Good afternoon!

Good evening!

2 Common Phrases

asking how someone is
How are you?
How are you today?
How are you doing?

express if you are not well
not bad, thanks.
not so good

phrases for meeting people
nice to meet you!
pleased to meet you!
It's a pleasure to meet you

Say how you are...
I'm fine. Thanks
I'm great!
I'm very well, thanks
I'm ok.

My name is Erick. What's your name?

My name is Manuel.

Psalms 5:3
Every *morning*, Lord, I lay my gifts before you and look to you for help. And every *morning* you hear my prayers.

Lesson 73

AT HOME

Who is God?
Write all the words or phrases you think of to describe God.
_____
_____
_____
_____

1 Write a formal conversation.

2 Write an informal conversation.

3 Practice the Phrases

informal greetings
_____
_____
_____

informal farewells
_____
_____
_____

formal greetings
_____
_____
_____
_____

ask how someone is
_____
_____
_____

say how you are
_____
_____
_____
_____

express if you are not well
_____
_____
_____

show pleasure to meet
_____
_____
_____

Practice greeting your classmates.
Make different dialogues.

Write Psalms 5:3
_____
_____
_____
_____
_____

Lesson 74

1 Reading Practice

I am Peter.
I am a disciple.
I am from Bethsaida.
I am a fisherman.
I work in a boat on the sea.

I am a man of God.
My name is Paul.
I am a tentmaker.
I am from Tarsus.
I am single.

Hi!
My name is Zacchaeus.
I am a tax collector.
I work for the emperor.

2 Dialogue 🎧 74.2

 *Hello. How are you doing? My name is Rosa.*

Nice to meet you Rosa. My name is Silvia.

 *I am from Nicaragua. Where are you from?*

I am from Japan. I am Japanese. but I live in Mexico. Where do you live?

I live in Managua with my family.

I have two children, a boy and a girl. What about you, are you married?

 *Yes, I am but I do not have children.*

Where do you work?

I work in a Call Center. Where do you work?

 *I am a secretary. I work in a big company.*

Practice greetings and introducing yourself with your classmates.

3 Personal Information

Where are you from?

I'm from <u>Honduras</u>.

Where do you come from?

I come from <u>Guatemala</u>.

Where do you live?

I live in <u>San Pedro Sula</u>.

Where do you work?

I work in <u>a small company</u>.

How old are you?

I'm <u>30</u> years old.

Are you married or single?

I'm married. / I'm single.

Do you have children?

Yes, I have <u>3</u> children. / No, I don't.

How long have you been a disciple?

I have been a disciple for <u>5</u> years.

Expressions to introduce yourself

My name is…
I'm…
Let me introduce myself, I'm..
I'd like to introduce myself, I'm..

Expressions to introduce others

Javier, please meet Luz.
Javier, have you met Carol?
I'd like you to meet Silvia.
I'd like to introduce you to Evlin.

Subject Pronouns	Verb To Be	Complement
I	am	a Christian.
You	are	from El Salvador.
We	are	Salvadorian.
They	are	my friends.
He	is	my father.
She	is	my mother.
It	is	my pet.

AT HOME

Lesson 75

1 Write and talk about them.

My name is _____.
I am from _____.
I am _____.
I am _____ years old.

Eric
Mexico

Peter
USA

My name is _____.
I am from _____.
I am _____.
I am _____ years old.

2 Personal Information

1.- Where are you from?
_____
2.- Where do you come from?
_____
3.- Where do you live?
_____
4.- What's your address?
_____
5.- Where do you work?
_____
6.- How old are you?
_____
7.- What´s your ID or passport number?
_____
8.- Are you married or single?
_____
9.- Do you have children?
_____
10. How long have you been a disciple?
_____

3 Give your address

My address is River Street, 7th avenue.
San Salvador, El Salvador.

My address is 9 Street, 1st avenue. San Pedro Sula, Honduras. Central America.

4 Write the words in the correct order.

1.- passport / what / number / is / your
_____?
2. married / are / you
_____?
3.- old / you / how / are
_____?
4.- you / where / from / are
_____?
5.- your / what / phone / is / number
_____?
6.- are / you / How
_____?
7.- children / do / have / you
_____?
8.- your / what / address / is
_____?
9.- live / where / you / do
_____?
10. work / you / where / do
_____?

Pretend you have a formal interview to apply for the following documents.

plane ticket   Identification Card   passport

5 Interview your friends.

Name	Age	Hometown	Lives in...

82

Lesson 76

Who is Jesus?

Matthew 16:16

Then Jesus said to his followers, "And who do you say I am?" Simon Peter answered, "You are the Messiah, the Son of the living God."

Complete:

Jesus is ____ Messiah, ____ son of ____ living God! Jesus is ____ Savior of the world.

1 THE NUMBERS 1-1000

1	one	21	twenty-one
2	two	30	thirty
3	three	31	thirty-one
4	four	40	forty
5	five	41	forty-one
6	six	50	fifty
7	seven	51	fifty-one
8	eight	60	sixty
9	nine	61	sixty-one
10	ten	70	seventy
11	eleven	71	seventy-one
12	twelve	80	eighty
13	thirteen	81	eighty-one
14	fourteen	90	ninety
15	fifteen	91	ninety-one
16	sixteen	100	one hundred
17	seventeen	200	two hundred
18	eighteen	300	three hundred
19	nineteen	400	four hundred
20	twenty	1000	one thousand

HOW MANY?

Is one of the words used for asking.
It asks for an exact number of objects.
It is used for countable nouns.

2 PRACTICE

I.- Practice saying the following numbers.

35 57 78 83 128 147 235 321
120 467 983 650 84 40 890 15

II.- Ask your classmates.

What's your phone number?

My phone number is 337-4561

What's your area code?

It's 603

3 Jesus feeds 5000 people

Discuss the following Bible Story in class.

Reference to John 6:10–14

There were about **5000** men who sat down there. Jesus took the loaves of bread and gave thanks for them. Then he gave them to the people. He did the same with the fish. He gave the people as much as they wanted. They all had plenty to eat.

The people had only **five** loaves of bread. But the followers filled **twelve** large baskets with the pieces of food that were left.

- How many loaves of bread did they have?
  They had _____ loaves of bread.

- How many people were fed?
  About _____ men were fed.

- How many baskets with leftovers were filled?
  _____ large baskets were filled with the pieces of food that were left.

Homework: Practice writing numbers.
Study numbers from 1-1000.

At Home

Lesson 77

1 Write the number word for each.

Number	Number word
112	
32	
71	
134	
50	
65	
174	
39	
147	
106	
341	
121	
136	
467	
964	
678	
506	
819	
314	
702	
529	
890	
456	
321	
953	
402	
208	
101	
222	
493	

2 Multiple Choice
Circle the correct number.

a) one hundred fifteen
   150   115   105

b) three hundred twelve
   302   320   312

c) thirty two
   320   32   30

d) seventy four
   704   74   84

e) ninety six
   96   69   90

f) six hundred fourteen
   640   614   416

g) nine hundred fifty seven
   967   975   957

h) eight hundred ninety four
   890   897   894

3 WORD SEARCH
Find the number word for each number.
Write the word on the line next to the number.

```
f i f t e e n c d r a g t
t e b s p r o f o r t y h
o c o e i g h t y a u c i
o t a v e i g h t e e n r
n h n e s e l e v e n m t
i r c n e d i t r f i v e
n e u t f o u r t e e n e
e e p y y c s i x t e e n
```

3 _____
40 _____
80 _____
15 _____
70 _____
9 _____
16 _____
13 _____
11 _____
25 _____
14 _____
18 _____

4 Write the number

a) three hundred fifty _____
b) one hundred nine _____
c) three hundred _____
d) six hundred eight _____
e) four hundred five _____
f) one hundred forty _____
g) seven hundred three _____
h) one hundred seven _____
i) seven hundred one _____
j) nine hundred three _____
k) eight hundred one _____
l) four hundred two _____
m) one thousand _____
n) seventeen _____
o) seventy _____
p) sixty eight _____
q) forty two _____
r) nineteen _____
s) fourteen _____
t) seven _____
u) fifteen _____
v) twelve _____
w) ninety _____
x) forty one _____

What number is this?

Matthew 18:21-22
Then Peter came to Jesus and asked, "Lord, when someone won't stop doing wrong to me, how many times must I forgive them? **seven** times?" Jesus answered, "I tell you, you must forgive them more than **seven** times. You must continue to forgive them even if they do wrong to you **seventy-seven** times."

Lesson 78

1 Talk about them. — SUBJECT PRONOUNS

(myself) I

Oscar Cabrera
Age: 30
Costa Rica

1) _____ am Oscar Cabrera.
2) _____ am 30 years old.
3) _____ am from Costa Rica.

(second person) YOU

Name: (your name)
age: (your age)
Country of origin:____

1) _____ are _____.
2) _____ are _____ years old.
3) _____ are from _____.

(another person and I) WE

Janine and I
married
El Salvador

1) _____ are Pablo and Janine.
2) _____ are married.
3) _____ are from El Salvador.

(2 or more people) THEY

David and Carlos
Age: 1
The USA

1) _____ are David and Carlos.
2) _____ are 1 year old.
3) _____ are from the USA.

Subject Pronouns

I	He
You	She
We	It
They	

(a boy, a man) HE

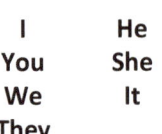
Ronaldo Rodriguez
age: 41
Guatemala

1) _____ is Ronaldo Rodriguez.
2) _____ is 41 years old.
3) _____ is from Guatemala.

(a girl, a woman) SHE

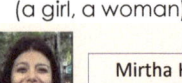
Mirtha Herrera
Age: 32
Managua

1) _____ is Mirtha Herrera.
2) _____ is 32 years old.
3) _____ is from Managua.

(an animal or thing) IT

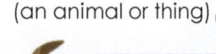
Benny
Age: 2 moths old

1) _____ is Benny.
2) _____ is two months old.
3) _____ is my pet.

2 ROLE PLAY

Pretend to be the following characters. Ask and answer questions about them with your classmates.

| A FAMOUS ACTOR | A FAMOUS ARTIST | THE PRESIDENT OF YOUR COUNTRY | AN EVANGELIST IN YOUR CHURCH | A FAMOUS ATHLETE |

3 READING

 My name is Mr. Escobar. I'm Honduran. I'm from Copan. My e-mail address is eco@net.com

 My name is Mrs. Bustillo. I'm American. I'm from California. My phone number is 367-5421. I'm 35 years old.

 My name is Mr. Zamboni. I'm from Guatemala. My license number is 4356.

 My name is Maria Guevara. My social security number is 31207. My apartment number is 48. My fax number is 2543-3092.

Titles in English:

| Mr. – a man | Mrs. – a married woman |
| Ms. – a woman (married or single) | Miss. – a single woman |

4 POSSESSIVE ADJECTIVES

HER
- What's her first name?
  Her first name is Ana.
- What's her middle name?
  Her middle name is Carola.
- What's her last name?
  Her last name is Bustillo.

HIS
- What's his first name?
  His first name is Erick.
- What's his middle name?
  His middle name is David.
- What's his last name?
  His last name is Escobar.

5 INTERVIEWS

Interview your classmates. Ask them about another person in the class.

First name	Middle name	Last name	Age

Homework: Cut out pictures of people from a magazine. Write their personal information. Share to the class.

Lesson 79

INTERVIEWS **At Home**

Interview friends or family. Then share with the rest of the class.

First name	Middle name	Last name	Age	Telephone number	E-mail address

SHE / HER

What's her age? How old is she?
Is she a disciple? Where is she from?
Is she married? Where does she work?
Is she a student?

HE / HIS

What's his age? How old is he?
Is he a disciple? Where is he from?
Is he married? Where does he work?
Is he a student?

LET'S TALK ABOUT...

Hi. My name's Daniel Lopez. I'm 10 years old. I'm a student. I live in Guatemala. I speak English.

What's his name? _____
What's his last name? _____
How old is he? _____
Where does he live? _____

What's his name? _____
How old is he? _____
Is he married? _____
Is he a disciple? _____
Is he a student? _____

Hello. My name's Gerardo Ulloa. I am 52 years old. I'm married and have two daughters. I live in San Pedro Sula, Honduras. I have been a disciple for 16 years. I am an ESOL student.

Hi. My name's Marlen Melendez. I'm 37 years old. I am a single mother. I have a son and a daughter. I live in Choloma. I have been a disciple for five years. I work for Hope Worldwide.

What's her name? _____
What's her last name? _____
What's her age? _____
Is she a mother? _____
Where does she work _____

What's her name? _____
How old is she? _____
Where is she from? _____
Where does she work? _____

Hi. My name's Juana Molina. I'm 44 years old. I am a single mother. I have a daughter. I am from Honduras. I live in Choloma. I work in an office. I have been a disciple for nineteen years.

Hello, My name's Maria Guevara. I'm 39 years old. I have been a disciple for seventeen years. I'm from Honduras. I live in La Lima, Cortes. I am single, and do not have children. I am a nurse and work for Hope Worldwide Honduras.

What's her name? _____
What's her last name? _____
How old is she? _____
Where's she from? _____
Where does she live? _____

Homework: Share your personal information with your classmates. Then, introduce three of your classmates to the rest of the class.

UNIT 7 SUMMARY

CONVERSATION
- What's your telephone number?
- My telephone number is ...
- What's your license number?
- My license number is ...
- What's your social security number?
- What's your apartment number?
- What's your address?
- Where do you live?
- Where do you work?
- Are you single / married?
- Do you have children?
- What's your age?

MEETING PEOPLE
- Hello.
- Hi
- What's your first name?
- My name is _____.
- What's your middle name?
- What's your last name?
- How are you today?
- Fine, thank you?
- How old are you?
- Nice to meet you!
- Nice to meet you, too.
- Where are you from?
- I'm from _____

VOCABULARY
- name
- first name
- middle name
- last name
- address
- e-mail address
- telephone number
- phone number
- cell phone number
- license number
- apartment number
- main street
- social security number
- fax number

GREETINGS
Formal greetings

Informal greetings

Farewells

NEW WORDS
savior
tent maker
tax collector
fisherman
sea
disciple

GRAMMAR

am	I'm from Guatemala.
is	What's your name? My name's Bessy.
Are	Where are you from? We're from Bolivia.

Subject	+ Verb + to Be	Complement
I	am	a Christian.
I	am	married.
You	are	good friends.
You	are	married.

Using Contractions
I'm a Christian.
I'm married.

You're good friends.
You're married.

Wh Words	+ Verb to Be	+ Poss. Adj.	+ Complement	Contraction
What	is	your	telephone number?	(What's...)
What	is	your	name?	(What's...)
What	is	your	nationality?	(What's...)
What	is	your	address?	(What's...)
Where	are	you	from?	

Using contractions

My name is Ted.   I am Pam.   His name is Chen.   I am from..
My name's Ted.   **I'm Pam.**   **His name's Chen.**   **I'm from..**

Subject Pronouns	Possessives Adjectives	Sentences
I	MY	My name's Jeannette.
YOU	YOUR	What's your address?
WE	OUR	These are our books.
THEY	THEIR	These are their notebooks.

Subject Pronouns	Possessives Adjectives	Sentences
HE	HIS	What's his address?
SHE	HER	This is her book.
IT	ITS	These are its colors.

UNIT 8

1ST ESOL TEACHER TRAINING

INTRODUCTION

In this unit, you will learn different countries and nationalities and will practice telling where people come from. You will also practice the use of possessive adjectives referring to people's belongings and also to people's relations and will review with them the subject pronouns.

Later, you will learn classroom object's vocabulary, classroom language and commands for you to start using them in your classroom.

You will also learn singular and plural demonstrative adjectives and Bible scriptures related to each topic.

OBJECTIVES

- Tell people's countries and nationalities..
- Use possessive adjectives to show people's belongings.
- Use possessive adjectives to show people's relations.
- Learn and use classroom object's vocabulary.
- Practice classroom language, and some classroom commands.
- Use singular and plural demonstrative adjectives.
- Learn different Bible Scriptures..

Countries and Nationalities

The USA / American 	Japan / Japanese 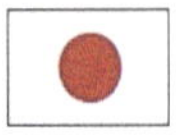	Honduras / Honduran 	Mexico / Mexican 	Brazil / Brazilian 
Canada / Canadian 	Guatemala / Guatemalan 	El Salvador / Salvadoran 	Germany / German 	Nicaragua / Nicaraguan 
Costa Rica / Costa Rican 	Chile / Chilean 	Puerto Rico / Puerto Rican 	Portugal / Portuguese 	Belize / Belizian 
South Africa / South African 	Israel / Israeli 	Venezuela / Venezuelan 	The United Kingdom / British 	Bolivia / Bolivian 
Greece / Greek 	Russia / Russian 	Spain / Spanish 	France / French 	Egypt / Egyptian 
Nigeria / Nigerian 	Australia / Australian 	Poland / Polish 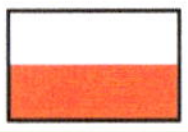	Ecuador / Ecuadorian 	Italy / Italian 
Cuba / Cuban 	Paraguay / Paraguayan 	Peru / Peruvian 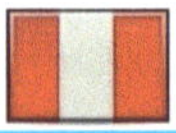	Uruguay / Uruguayan 	Argentina / Argentinian 
Panama / Panamanian 	Ireland / Irish 	China / Chinese 	Colombia / Colombian 	Jamaica / Jamaican 

WHERE ARE YOU FROM?

1.- I'm from _____.
2.- You're from _____.
3.- We're from _____.
4.- They're from _____.
5.- He's from _____.
6.- She's from _____.
7.- It's from _____.

WHAT'S YOUR NATIONALITY?

My nationality is _____.
Your nationality is _____.
Our nationality is _____.
Their nationality is _____.
His nationality is _____.
Her nationality is _____.
Its nationality is _____.

Lesson 81

AT HOME

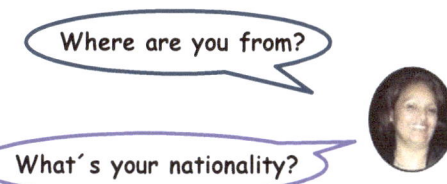

- Where are you from?
- What's your nationality?
- I'm from Turkey.
- I'm Italian.

1 PRACTICE

Chen / Peru
Where's Chen from?
She's from _____.
What's **her** nationality?
She's _____.

Pancho / Costa Rica
Where's Pancho from?
He's from _____.
What's **his** nationality?
He's _____.

Eduardo / Panama
Where's Eduardo from?
He's from _____.
What's **his** nationality?
He's _____.

Claudia / Guatemala
Where're Claudia and Brenda from?
They're from _____.
What's **their** nationality?
They're _____.

2 ANSWER

Read the dialogue and place a check mark (✓) to the correct option.

Sue : Hi! My name is Sue. What's your name?
Keiko : My name is Keiko.
Sue : Well, hello Keiko. Are you Chinese?
Keiko : No, I am not. I'm Japanese. Are you English, Sue?
Sue : Yes, I am. I'm from England.
Keiko : How old are you, Sue?
Sue : I'm fifteen years old. How about you?
Keiko : I'm fourteen years old.

	YES	NO
1.- Keiko is Chinese.	☐	☐
2.- Sue is fifteen years old.	☐	☐
3.- Sue is from England.	☐	☐
4.- Keiko is from Japan.	☐	☐
5.- Keiko is fourteen years old.	☐	☐

SEVEN CONTINENTS

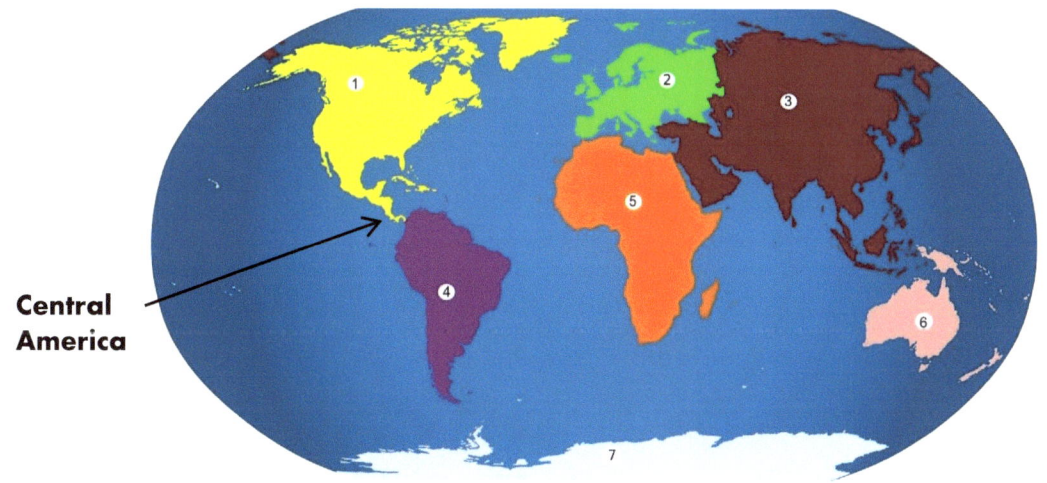

Central America

1. North America
2. Europe
3. Asia
4. South America
5. Africa
6. Australia
7. Antarctica

Homework: Study the list of countries and their nationalities.

Lesson 82

WHERE ARE YOU FROM?

 My name is Luz. I am from Managua, Nicaragua. I'm Nicaraguan.

 My name's Mirtha. I am from Cuba. I'm Cuban.

 My name is Paulo. I am from China. I'm Chinese.

 I'm Edwin. I'm from Japan. I'm Japanese.

1 Practice with your classmates

What's your name? **Where are you from?** **What's your nationality?**

| Jose / Canada | Carlos / Mexico | Benito / Brazil | Mirna / Guatemala |
| Jen / Brazil | Pat / Cuba | Sam / The USA | Denia / Italy | Luz / Egypt |

What's his name? **Where is he from?** **What's his nationality?**

| Javier Gonzales / Honduras | Carlos / Mexico | Benito / Brazil | Allan Xavier / Guatemala |
| Hector Pinto / Brazil | Manuel Saso / Cuba | Lester Luna / Italy | Fernando Lopez / Egypt |

2 Practice

- What's her name?
  Her name is Tania.
- Where's she from?
  She's from Canada.
- What's her nationality?
  She's Canadian.

 Tania Sian — Canada
 Jenny Galeano — Brazil
 Jeannette — Mexico
 Mayra — Chile
 Dulce Cruz — The USA

- What are our names?
  Our names are Marie and Allan.
- Where are we from?
  We're from Honduras.
- What's our nationality?
  We're Honduran.

 Marie and Allan — Honduras
 Indira and Aryany — Canada
 Mary and Danilo — Chile
 Dominga and Gerardo — Jamaica

- What are their names?
  Their names are Wendy and Bill.
- Where are they from?
  They're from Peru.
- What's their nationality?
  They're Peruvian.

 Wendy and Bill — Peru
 Lori and Walter — Germany
 Alex and Andrea — Colombia
 Hector and Dulce — Argentina

Homework: Write about 6 famous people, tell what country they come from and their nationalities.

Lesson 83

AT HOME

1 WHERE ARE WE FROM?

Write about the following people, tell their names, where they come from and their nationalities.

Name	Country	Nationality
Daniel and I / Nicaragua	Diana and I / Jamaica	Salvadora and I / Europe
Jacqueline and I / Bolivia	Kevin and I / Spain	Mauricio and I / Israel

WHERE ARE THEY FROM?

Name	Country	Nationality
Allan and Sharon / Portugal	Jose Andres and Miurel / Belize	Maritza and Kevin / Russia
Beira and Christofer / Cuba	Deysi and Thais / Costa Rica	Fredy and Edgard / Greek

2 READ

Read. Then, answer the questions.

My friends at church are very interesting. Fredy Hernandez is Spanish. He's from Madrid. Dominga and her husband are Chinese. They're from Shanghai. Ramiro and Carola are from Egypt. They're Egyptian. Brenda and her daughters are from Germany. They're German. Flor and her mother are from Italy. We all come from so many different countries and we're friends. We are more than friends. We are a big family!

Answer:

1. Where are Brenda and her daughters from?   They're from _____. They're _____.
2. Where's Fredy Hernandez from?   He's from _____. He's _____.
3. Where are Flor and her mother from?   They're from _____. They're _____.
4. Where are Dominga and her husband from?   They're from _____. They're _____.
5. Where are Ramiro and Carola from?   They're from _____. They're _____.

3 WRITING

- Write your family's personal information, name, ID number, telephone number, address, e-mail address, and driver's license.
- Find out where your classmates come from and write about it. Include their city and nationality.

The Acts 10:35 (ICB)

God accepts anyone who worships him and does what is right. It is not important what country a person comes from.

Homework: Write about 6 famous people, tell what country they come from and what are their nationalities.

Lesson 84

Let's talk about ...

1 Building a Tower

🎧 84.1 **Listen to the Scripture. Discuss it in class.**

Genesis 11:1-9

There was a time when the whole world spoke one language. Everyone used the same words.

Then people said to each other, "Let's build ourselves a city and a tower that will reach to the sky. Then we will be famous. This will keep us together so that we will not be scattered all over the earth."

Then the LORD came down to see the city and the tower.

The LORD said, "These people all speak the same language. And I see that they are joined together to do this work. Let's go down and confuse their language. Then they will not understand each other." So people stopped building the city, and the LORD scattered them all over the earth.

That is the place where the LORD confused the language of the whole world. That is why it is called Babel. The LORD caused the people to spread out to all the other places on earth.

New Words:
_____ _____ _____
_____ _____ _____

Answer
1. What was the name of the city?
2. What were the men building?
3. Why did they want to build that tower?
4. Did God like what they were doing?
5. What did God do?
6. What do you think about it?

2 Landmarks Around The World

Paris

Eiffel Tower
The Eiffel Tower is the most recognizable landmark in Paris and is known worldwide as a symbol of France. Named after its designer, Gustave Eiffel, it is a premier tourist destination, with over 5.5 million visitors per year.

India

Taj Mahal
In 1631 the emperor Shan Jahan built the Taj Mahal in memory of his wife, who died in childbirth. This building is considered the most beautiful building in the world.

China

The Great Wall of China
The Chinese worked on the Great Wall for over 1700 years. In turn, each emperor who came to power added pieces of the wall to protect their empire.

Honduras

Copan Ruins
The Ruins in Copan, Honduras belong to one of the greatest ancient Mayan Cultures. It is visited for many people from all around the globe.

Guatemala

Tikal Ruins
Tikal is a city of Mayan ruins located in Guatemala. Tikal was a very important and influential city. Like the rest of the great Maya cities, Tikal fell into decline around 900 A.D. It is currently an important archaeological and tourism site.

Answer

- What country would you like to live in? Why?
  I would like to live in _____ because_____.

- What country would you like to visit? Why?
  I would like to visit _____ because_____.

- What countries have you been to?
  I have been to _____.

- Do you have friends in other countries?
  Yes, I do. / No, I don't.

- What other languages would you like to learn?
  I would like to learn _____ and _____.

- Why would you like to learn these languages?
  I would like to learn _____ and _____ because_____.

Lesson 85

Why to study the Bible?
2 Timothy 3:16

All Scripture is given by God. And all Scripture is useful for teaching and for showing people what is wrong in their lives. It is useful for correcting faults and teaching the right way to live.

Answer:
Do you believe in God?
Do you believe in the Bible as the Word of God?
Do you study the Bible every day?

Demonstrative Adjectives

This, That / These, Those

What´s this?   What´s that?
This is a Bible.   That´s a pen.

What are these?   What are those?
These are markers.   Those are papers.

Practice with different school objects.

Complete the ideas:

1. _____ is the word of God.
I must study the Bible every day.

2. _____ book has the Power to change my life.

3. _____ is a wonderful book to learn about God.

4. Is _____ amazing book changing my life already?

CLASSROOM OBJECTS

- pencil
- pen
- crayons
- colored pencils
- paper
- book
- ruler
- school bag
- calculator
- scissors
- notebook
- eraser
- blackboard
- pencil sharpener
- folder
- pencil case
- desk
- computer
- glue
- board
- globe
- chair

- classroom
- hole punch
- ballpoint pen
- stapler
- staples
- compass
- magnifying glass
- clips
- thumbtacks
- rubber band
- mechanical pencil
- portfolio
- CD player
- chalk
- cardboard
- stickers
- nametag
- glitter
- teacher
- student
- map
- clock

Homework: Study the list of classroom objects.

SINGULAR

This
Affirmative: This is my folder.
Negative: This is not my folder.
Interrogative: Is this my folder?

That
Affirmative: That is my folder.
Negative: That is not my folder.
Interrogative: Is that my folder?

PLURAL

These
Affirmative: These are my stickers.
Negative: These are not my stickers.
Interrogative: Are these my stickers?

Those
Affirmative: Those are my stickers.
Negative: Those are not my stickers.
Interrogative: Are those my stickers?

 **This** is my pencil.   **That** is my pencil.

 **These** are my pencils.   **Those** are my pencils.

Lesson 86

AT HOME

1 WHAT'S THIS?

Work in pairs. Ask a classmate what the objects are. Then circle the correct answer.

a) scissors   c) folder
b) schoolbag d) book

a) backpack   c) stapler
b) dictionary d) map

a) pencil case c) eraser
b) dictionary d) crayons

a) pencil case c) ruler
b) notebook   d) chalk

a) sharpeners c) pens
b) book cases d) chairs

a) blackboard c) eraser
b) file folder d) bin

a) pencil case c) ruler
b) notebook   d) paper

a) paper clip c) pencil
b) rubber band d) glue

a) hole punch c) stapler
b) computer   d) book

a) chalkboard c) window
b) desk   d) door

a) push pins   c) staplers
b) erasers   d) folders

a) globe   c) compass
b) scissors   d) paper clip

a) compass   c) desk
b) sticker   d) clock

a) notebook   c) pencil
b) desk   d) chair

a) computer   c) map
b) sticker   d) eraser

a) sharpeners c) folders
b) notebooks   d) boards

a) calculators c) stickers
b) lunchboxes d) laptops

a) pushpin   c) scissors
b) lunchbox   d) map

a) door   c) table
b) board   d) chair

a) dictionary c) book
b) computer   d) Bible

a) ballpoint pen c) desk
b) eraser   d) scissors

a) laptop   c) desk
b) clock   d) door

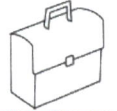
a) schoolbag   c) bin
b) lunchbox   d) paper

a) hole punch c) pens
b) stickers   d) pencils

Homework: Study the list of classroom objects. Practice writing them at home.

Lesson 87

Let's talk about ...

THE CLASSROOM

- How is your classroom?
- How many classmates do you have?
- Are all of them your friends?
- Where do they come from?

Proverbs 4:1 (ICB)
Children, listen to your father's teaching. Pay attention so you will understand.

Proverbs 2:4-5
Look for wisdom like silver. Search for it like hidden treasure. If you do this, you will understand what it means to respect the LORD, and you will come to know God.

Proverbs 17:10
Smart people learn more from a single correction than fools learn from a hundred beatings.

Philippians 4:13
I can do all things through him who strengthens me.

SCHOOL OBJECTS

Think about the school objects vocabulary.

- How many of these items do you know?
- How many of these are new for you?

- Look around your classroom. Which items do you see?
- How many of these objects do you use every day?
- Which ones does your teacher use most often?
- What items do you carry in your book bag?
- What items do your classmates carry in their book bags?

The ESOL Program

ESOL BACKGROUND

In the year 2009 Hope Worldwide started sending teams of volunteers to San Pedro Sula, Honduras, and the leaders quickly became aware of the need for more bilingual speakers (Spanish/English). Few members of the church were able to speak English, so translators were scarce. Children of ICOC church members who attended bilingual schools were often asked to translate for the volunteers. As a result of the great need to learn English, the HOPE worldwide Community Service Brigade program raises the funding in the U.S. to hire an English teacher and purchases the curriculum and supplies needed to start-up the first ESOL class in Central America for the brothers and sisters of the San Pedro Sula Church.

Why do you need to learn English?

TRAVEL

BETTER JOB

MAKE WORLDWIDE FRIENDS

UNDERSTAND LITERATURE

HELP OTHERS

BETTER POSITION IN YOUR JOB

COMMUNICATE

TO BE A TRANSLATOR

USE THE WEB

Lesson 88

1 POSSESSIVE ADJECTIVES

Practice each possessive adjectives.

Subject Pronoun	Possessive Adjectives
I	my
You	your
We	our
They	their
He	his
She	her
It	its

My name is Skarlet. Is this your schoolbag?

Psalms 119:2
Great blessings belong to those who follow **his** rules! They seek him with all **their** heart.

Psalms 119:18
Open **my** eyes so that I can see all the wonderful things in **your** teachings.

Psalms 119:10
I try with all my heart to serve you. Help me obey **your commands**.

Psalms 119:35
Help me follow **your commands**, because that makes me happy.

Talk about the scripture
1.- What do you think about these scriptures?
2.- What are some of God's commands?

1. Possessive adjectives are used to show possession or ownership.

2. The possessive adjective needs to agree with the person or owner.

2 Ask about the objects below. Write the correct possessive adjective on the line provided.

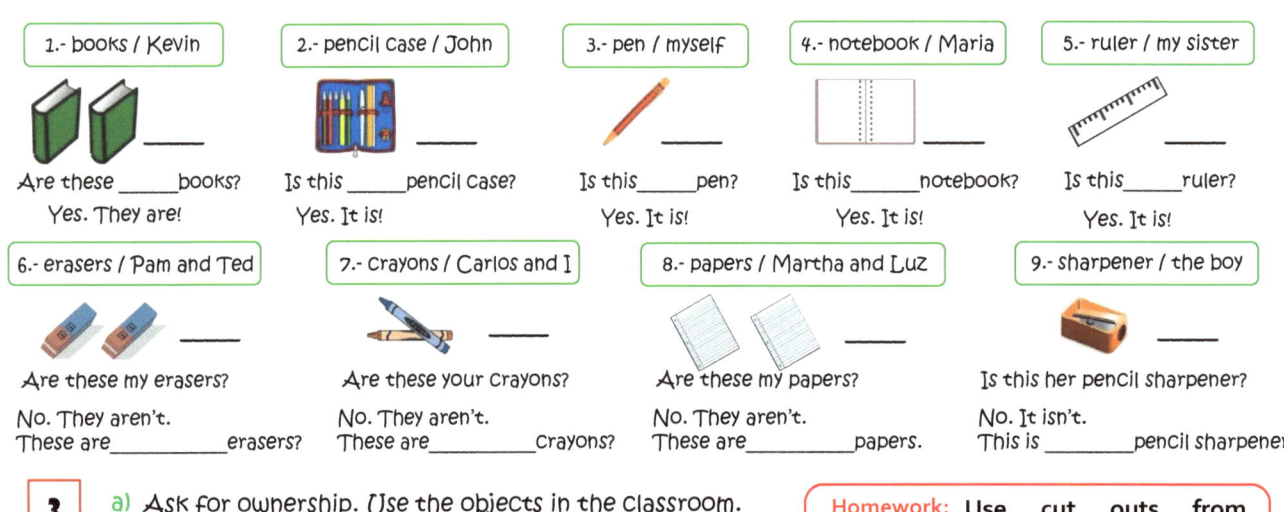

1.- books / Kevin
Are these _____ books?
Yes. They are!

2.- pencil case / John
Is this _____ pencil case?
Yes. It is!

3.- pen / myself
Is this _____ pen?
Yes. It is!

4.- notebook / Maria
Is this _____ notebook?
Yes. It is!

5.- ruler / my sister
Is this _____ ruler?
Yes. It is!

6.- erasers / Pam and Ted
Are these my erasers?
No. They aren't.
These are _____ erasers?

7.- Crayons / Carlos and I
Are these your crayons?
No. They aren't.
These are _____ crayons?

8.- papers / Martha and Luz
Are these my papers?
No. They aren't.
These are _____ papers.

9.- sharpener / the boy
Is this her pencil sharpener?
No. It isn't.
This is _____ pencil sharpener.

3
a) Ask for ownership. Use the objects in the classroom.

b) Give examples of people in the classroom and their belongings. Use the correct possessive adjectives.

Homework: Use cut outs from magazines to talk about famous people and their belongings.

4 Commands

1. A command is an instruction given.
2. A command does not need a subject. e.g. You sit down please!

Practice each command.

- ☐ Sit down please!
- ☐ Clean the board!
- ☐ Come to the board!
- ☐ Close the door please.
- ☐ Open your book to pg. 25
- ☐ Close your book.
- ☐ Pay attention.

- ☐ Repeat the words please.
- ☐ Do your homework.
- ☐ Raise your hand.
- ☐ Work together.
- ☐ Read...
- ☐ Listen...
- ☐ Be quiet please!

Hi! **My** name is Dominga. This is **my** family. **They** are Camila and Sofia. **He** is **my** husband. **His** name is Gerardo Ulloa. **He** is 52 years old.

Homework: Study the list of commands.
Cut out pictures of famous people from a magazine. Write and talk about their belongings.

Lesson 89

AT HOME

1 Decide whether to use a subject pronoun or a possessive pronoun where is needed.

I / my
My name is _____.
_____ last name is _____.
_____ am from _____.
_____ am ____ years old.
_____ friends are from Cuba.
_____ family is from _____.

You / your
_____ name is Andrea.
_____ last name is Diaz.
_____ are from Canada.
_____ are 35 years old.
_____ are married.
_____ phone number is 35218.

We / our
_____ are friends.
_____ are disciples.
_____ friends are disciples too.
_____ are from Mexico.
_____ friends are from Tegucigalpa.
_____ are single.

They / their
_____ names are Zuly and Silvia.
_____ are friends.
_____ are from Bolivia.
_____ are single.
_____ friends are single too.

He / his
_____ name is Angel.
_____ last name is Rodriguez.
_____ is from Chicago.
_____ is 22 years old.
_____ is married.

She / her
_____ name is Rosario.
_____ last name is Muñoz.
_____ is from Peru.
_____ is 18 years old.
_____ is single.

2 Complete using a subject pronoun or a possessive pronoun.

Carlos David (They)
1) What are _____ names?
_____ names are Carlos and David.
2) Where are _____ from?
_____ are from Boston.
3) How old are _____?
_____ are 9 years old.

Ismael and I (We)
1) What are _____ names?
_____ names are Tom and Luis.
2) Where are _____ from?
_____ are from Nicaragua
3) How old are _____?
_____ are 10 years old.

Gatty (He)
1) What is _____ name?
_____ name is Gatty.
2) Where is _____ from?
_____ is from Honduras.
3) How old is _____?
_____ is three months old.

Rosa (She)
1) What is _____ name?
_____ name is Rosa.
2) Where is _____ from?
_____ is from El Salvador.
3) How old is _____?
_____ is 15 years old.

3 TALK ABOUT THEM

Write about each person. Use the correct subject pronouns and possessive adjectives for each.

Rafael

Deysi

Javier

Jesus

Homework: Cut out pictures of famous people from a magazine. Write about them. Then, share to the class.

Lesson 90

1. CLASSROOM LANGUAGE (90.1)

Practice the phrases.

- Can I go to the toilet please?
- May I get a drink of water?
- Excuse me, I don´t understand.
- Can you repeat that please?
- Could you say that again please?
- Sorry, I´m late.
- How do you spell___?
- How do you say _____ in English?
- What´s the word for_____ in English?
- How do you pronounce_____?
- May I sharpen my pencil?
- I´m sorry, I don´t understand!
- What´s the meaning of ¨table¨?
- Can I clean the board?

*Repeat each phrase or sentence.
Practice with a classmate.*

Proverbs 13:1
A wise son **listens** to his father's advice, but a proud son will not **listen to** correction.

Job 5:9-10
People cannot **understand** the wonderful things God does. His miracles are too many to count. He does things too marvelous for people to **understand**. He does too many miracles to count!

Proverbs 28:9
When people do not **listen** to God's **teachings**, he does not **listen** to their prayers.

WHO?
Is one of the words used for asking. It asks for the person who performs a certain action.

POSSESSIVE ADJECTIVES REFERRING TO PEOPLE

Possessive adjectives are used to refer to people in the sense of their relationships.

2. PRACTICE THE DIALOGUE (90.2)

Susan: Hello Luis! How are you today?
Luis: Hi Susan! I'm fine. Thank you. What about you?
Susan: I'm a little worried about my English lessons.
Luis: Oh! Really! I can help you if you want.
Susan: Yes, please! I sometimes do not understand the words.
Luis: Oh.. In that case you could tell the teacher "Excuse me, I don't understand. Could you please repeat that word?"
Susan: Okay. And if I don't know how to pronounce a word, what can I say?
Luis: You say.. "How do you pronounce that word?"
Susan: Oh.. Thank you so much!
Luis: You're welcome!

1.- WHO IS HE?

Who is he?
He's my father.
What's his name?
His name is Paul.

2.- WHO IS __SHE__?   WHAT IS __HER__ NAME?

my mother
Julissa

my father
Jorge

my sister
Kate

3.- WHO ARE THEY?   WHAT ARE THEIR NAMES?

Our parents
Jim and Sue

Tom and his
brother Carlos

Kate and her
friend Bill

Homework: Bring pictures of your family or cut out pictures of famous people and their families. Write and talk about the relationships.

AT HOME

Lesson **91**

1 WORD ORDER
Write the words in order to make questions and answer them.

1. names / what / are / their?
   _____
   a) _____

2. from / they / where / are?
   _____
   a) _____

3. its / name / is / what?
   _____
   a) _____

4. we / where / from / are?
   _____
   a) _____

5. What / their / are / numbers / telephone?
   _____
   a) _____

6. last name / your / is / what?
   _____
   a) _____

2 Replace the underline noun (s) with the correct subject pronoun. Then, rewrite the sentence.

1) The man is from Guatemala.
   _____
2) The woman is my friend.
   _____
3) The children are in the house.
   _____
4) Raffy and Jose Luis are my best friends.
   _____
5) The dog is my pet Rex.
   _____
6) The boys are my children.
   _____
7) Susan and I are from Venezuela.
   _____

3 Decide whether to use subject pronouns or possessive adjectives to complete the ideas.

1.- Maria is from Cuba. _____ is 10 years old. _____ mother is from El Salvador. _____ sister is from Managua.

2.- Marcos is a teacher. _____ is from The USA. _____ brother Juan is from The USA too. _____ parents are from Costa Rica.

3.- Taly and Ted are brothers. _____ are from Chile. _____ older brother, Carlos is from Peru. _____ parents are from Mexico.

4 Write about people in your class. Use possessive adjectives correctly.

1. _____
   _____
   _____

2. _____
   _____
   _____

5 Choose the correct word from the parentheses to complete the sentences. Then, rewrite them.

1. (He/His) is from Xelaju. (He/His) is Guatemalan.
   _____

2. (Her/She) is a student. (Her/She) is my friend.
   _____

3. (They/Their) are Tom and Jorge. (They/Their) are from China.
   _____

4. (We/Our) are married. (We/Our) are happy.
   _____

5. I have a dog. (It/Its) name is Rexy.
   _____

6. Where is (you/your) mother from?
   _____

7. (She/Her) is from Japan. (She/Her) is Japanese.
   _____

Lesson 92

Let's talk about ...
Jesus meets a woman in Samaria

 John 4:3

Jesus goes to Galilee. On his way, he goes through the country of Samaria. Jesus, tired from his long trip, comes to a well and sits down. A Samaritan woman comes to the well to get some water, and Jesus asks her for water. She is surprised about this because Jews have nothing to do with Samaritans.

Jesus says "You don't know who I am. If you knew, you would have asked me for water, and I would have given you living water."

The woman asked, "Are you greater than our ancestor Jacob? He is the one who gave us this well." Jesus answered, "Everyone who drinks this water will be thirsty again. But anyone who drinks the water I give will never be thirsty again.

The water I give people will be like a spring flowing inside them. It will bring them eternal life."

New Words:
_____ _____ _____
_____ _____ _____

Circle the subject pronouns in color **red**.
Underline the possessive adjectives in color **blue**.

Complete:
Jesus goes to_____
Jesus sits down beside the_____
Jesus meets a_____
The woman is from_____
Jesus asks the woman for_____
Jesus offers her_____

Choose the correct answer

1.- _____ meets a woman from_____.
a) God   b) Jesus   c) Samaria

2.- The woman tells Jesus he does not have anything to get _____ with.
a) life   b) faith   c) water

3.- Jesus offers her _____.
a) living water   b) fresh water   c) bread

The Names of God

The God of Israel
2 Chronicles 6:7
Isaiah 48:2

The LORD All-Powerful
Isaiah 47:4
Isaiah 48:2

The Holy One of Israel
Isaiah 47:4

The God of your ancestors-the God of Abraham, the God of Isaac, the God of Jacob
Exodus 3:15

Answer
I.- What are some of the names given to God?
1.- _____
2.- _____
3.- _____
4.- _____
5.- _____
6.- _____

The Names of Jesus

The Son of God
Mark 1:1
Colossians 1:14

The Messiah
Mark 1:1
John 11:27

Jesus Christ
2 Corinthians 1:19

The Light of the World
John 8:12

Answer
I.- What are some of the names given to Jesus?
1.- _____
2.- _____
3.- _____
4.- _____

II.- What do you think about the scriptures?
_____
_____

Homework:
Listen to the Bible story at home.
Learn new words.

UNIT 8 SUMMARY

DEFINITE ARTICLES
THE
- the pencil
- the orange

INDEFINITE ARTICLES
A — a strawberry
AN — an orange

7 CONTINENTS
- North America
- South America
- Europe
- Asia
- Africa
- Australia
- Antarctica

CLASSROOM LANGUAGE
- Can I go to the bathroom please?
- May I get a drink of water?
- Excuse me, I don't understand.
- Can you repeat that please?
- Could you say that again please?
- Sorry, I'm late.
- How do you spell___?
- How do you say ____ in English?
- What's the word for____ in English?
- How do you pronounce____?
- May I sharpen my pencil?
- I'm sorry, I don't understand!
- What's the meaning of table?
- Can I clean the board please?

CLASSROOM COMMANDS
- Sit down!
- Clean the board!
- Come to the board!
- Close the door please.
- Open your book to pg. 25
- Close your book.
- Pay attention.
- Repeat the words please.
- Do your homework.
- Raise your hand.
- Work together.
- Write…
- Read…
- Be quiet please!

COUNTRIES AND NATIONALITIES

Country	Nationality
Honduras	Honduran
Mexico	Mexican
El Salvador	Salvadoran
Nicaragua	Nicaraguan
Guatemala	Guatemalan
Latin America	Latin American
Canada	Canadian
Australia	Australian
Cuba	Cuban
Egypt	Egyptian
Spain	Spanish
France	French
Greece	Greek
Russia	Russian
China	Chinese
Japan	Japanese
Brazil	Brazilian
Italy	Italian
Poland	Polish
Ireland	Irish
Portugal	Portuguese
Nigeria	Nigerian
Israel	Israeli
Colombia	Colombian

CLASSROOM OBJECTS

pencil	notebook	cardboard	Pen
crayons	eraser	mechanical pencil	Paper
book	blackboard	Classroom	chalk
ruler	folder	pencil sharpener	globe
desk	pencil case	hole punch	stickers
calculator	compass	ballpoint pen	nametag
Scissors	school bag	colored pencils	glitter
portfolio	computer	magnifying glass	teacher
CD player	glue	rubber band	stapler
Student	Board	thumbtacks	staples
map	clock	rubber band	Clips

DEMONSTRATIVE ADJECTIVES

This	These
This is my pencil.	These are my pens.
This isn't my pencil.	These aren't my pens.
Is this my pencil?	Are these my pens?

That	Those
That is your book.	Those are my books.
That isn't your book.	Those aren't my books.
Is that your book?	Are those my books?

POSSESSIVE ADJECTIVES

Subject Pronoun	Possessive Adjectives	Sentences
I	my	My name is Mirna.
You	your	Your nationality is Cuban.
We	our	Our friends come from El Salvador.
They	their	Their names are Catarino and Kevin.
He	his	His mother is Maria Teresa.
She	her	Her sister is American.
It	its	The dog has its big bone.

UNIT 9

ESOL CLASS - GUATEMALA

INTRODUCTION

In this unit, you will be able to tell the color and shape of objects and things as well as describe nouns using opposite adjectives. You will read story of Daniel and his friends and will be able to identify the adjectives in the story.

Later, you will use prepositions of place to tell where the objects or the people are. You will discover how to write the plural of different nouns and also be able to use those nouns in daily speech correctly.

Finally, you will review prepositions of place and plural nouns through the story of the creation of God, and also learn how to write and use ordinal numbers.

OBJECTIVES

- Use colors and shapes to describe nouns.
- Describe objects and people using opposite adjectives.
- Learn the story of Daniel and his friends.
- Use prepositions of place to show location of objects and people.
- Learn the rules to write plural nouns.
- Talk about the Creation of God.
- Write ordinal numbers from 1 to 20.

Lesson 93

Why is it important to pray?

Mark 1:35

The next morning Jesus woke up very early. He left the house while it was still dark and went to a place where he could be alone and pray.

Colossians 4:2

Never stop praying. Be ready for anything by praying and being thankful.

1 🎧 93.1 **SHAPES** *What shape is this?*

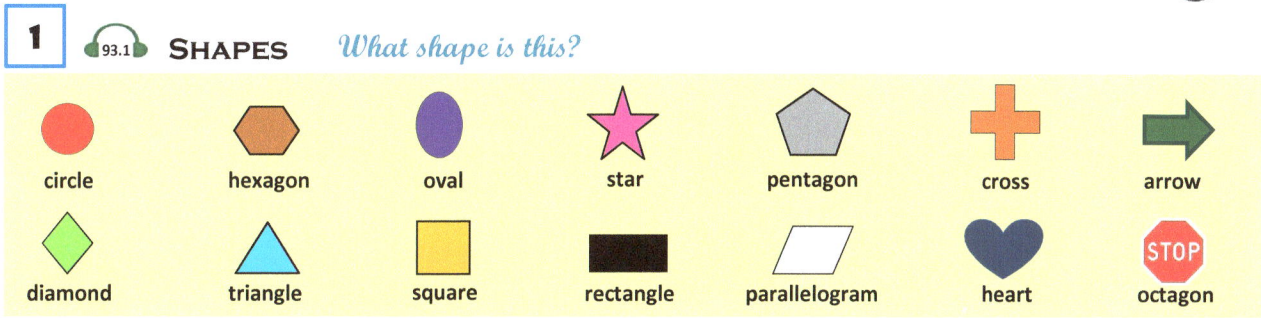

2 🎧 93.2 **COLORS** *What color is this?*

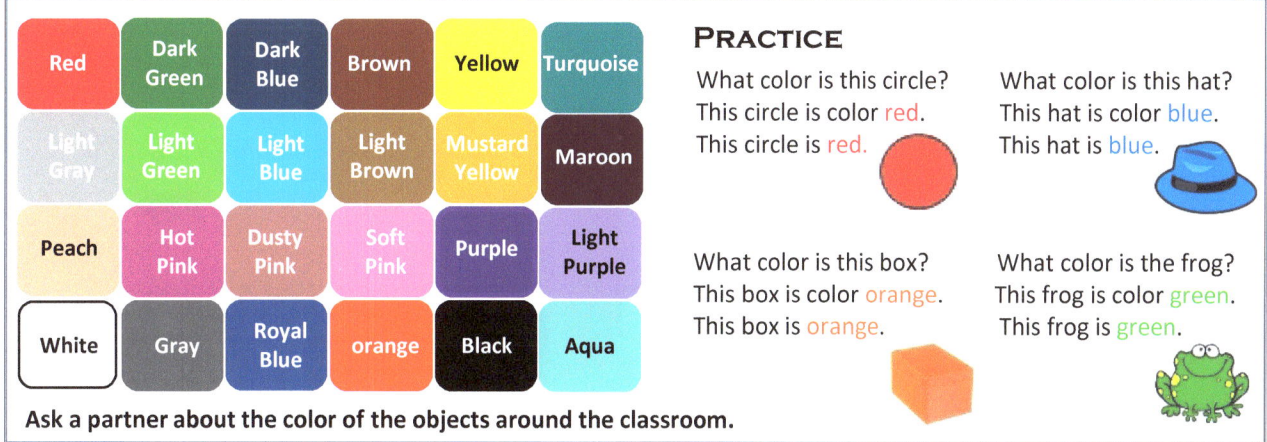

Ask a partner about the color of the objects around the classroom.

Homework: Write sentences describing the shapes and colors of nouns.

3 **DESCRIBING NOUNS** *What color is this balloon?*

balloon

dog

grapes

house

chair

pillow

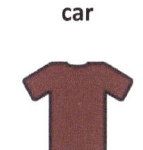

car

T-shirt

butterfly

flower

cap

shoes

Lesson 94

OPPOSITE ADJECTIVES I

Adjectives are words that describe nouns.

young

How is the boy?
The boy is young.
He is a young boy.

happy

How is the clown?
The clown is happy.
He is a happy clown.

hot

How is the weather?
The weather is hot.
It is a hot day.

cold

How is the weather?
The weather is cold.
It's a cold day.

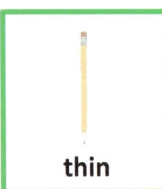
thin

How is the yellow pencil?
The yellow pencil is thin.
It is a thin pencil.

thick

How is the yellow pencil?
The yellow pencil is thick.
It's a thick pencil.

big

How is the stone?
The stone is big.
It's a big stone.

small

How is the stone?
The stone is small.
It's a small stone.

1. Opposite Adjectives
Repeat each pair of opposite adjectives.

1. high	low	11. strong	weak
2. wet	dry	12. pretty	ugly
3. near	far	13. big	small
4. quiet	loud	14. fast	slow
5. cold	hot	15. young	old
6. clean	dirty	16. new	old
7. good	bad	17. happy	sad
8. left	right	18. enormous	tiny
9. dark	light	19. tall	short
10. heavy	light	20. clever	dumb

Sentence Structure

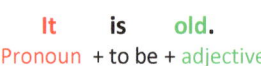

The car is old.
Noun + to be + adjective

It is old.
Pronoun + to be + adjective

It is an old car.
Pronoun + to be + article + adj. + noun

The car is new.
Noun + to be + adjective

It is new.
Pronoun + to be + adjective

It is a new car.
Pronoun + to be + article + adj. + noun

Examples:

Luis is a strong man.
The man is strong.
He is strong.

It is a slow bike.
The bike is slow.
It is slow.

It is a fast ambulance.
The ambulance is fast.
It is fast.

2. Practice
Describe the objects using the adjectives in parentheses.

dictionary
(good, new, heavy)

bed
(soft, small, old)

umbrella
(pretty, clean, light)

television
(old, ugly)

house
(big, new)

church
(big, old)

Roberto
(happy, clever, quiet)

tree
(tall, old)

Homework: Describe nouns using opposite adjectives.

Lesson 95

AT HOME

1 Label
Label the colors.

_____ _____ _____

_____ _____ _____

_____ _____ _____

4 Match
Write the number of the opposite adjective on the line provided.

___ light	1. high	___ slow	11. strong
___ loud	2. wet	___ dumb	12. pretty
___ hot	3. near	___ low	13. big
___ low	4. quiet	___ old	14. fast
___ dirty	5. cold	___ sad	15. young
___ bad	6. clean	___ weak	16. new
___ right	7. good	___ ugly	17. happy
___ dry	8. left	___ small	18. old
___ far	9. dark	___ young	19. tall
___ light	10. heavy	___ short	20. clever

2 Write
Write sentences using adjectives.

1.- _____
2.- _____
3.- _____
4.- _____
5.- _____
6.- _____
7.- _____
8.- _____

5 Label
Label the shapes.

_____ _____ _____

_____ _____ _____

_____ _____ _____

3 Write
Use the adjectives in parentheses to describe the objects.

bed (soft/small) _____

television (old/heavy) _____

house (big, new) _____

umbrella (pretty / expensive) _____

What's your favorite color?
_____

Lesson 96

OPPOSITE ADJECTIVES II

Practice the use of adjectives in affirmative and negative form.

cheap

This ring is cheap.
It is not expensive.

expensive

This ring is expensive.
It is not cheap.

empty

The glass is empty.
It is not full.

full

The glass is full.
It is not empty.

bitter

The lemon is bitter.
It is not sweet.

sweet

This cake is sweet.
It is not bitter.

long

This snake is long.
It is not short.

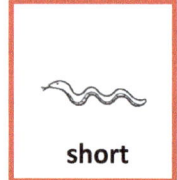
short

This snake is short.
It is not long.

1. Opposites 96.1
Repeat each pair of opposite adjectives.

1.-	empty	full	11.- long	short
2.-	deep	shallow	12.- polite	impolite
3.-	cheap	expensive	13.- true	false
4.-	right	wrong	14.- thin	fat
5.-	clear	dark	15.- early	late
6.-	ugly	beautiful	16.- narrow	wide
7.-	rich	poor	17.- angry	calm
8.-	easy	difficult	18.- in	out
9.-	safe	dangerous	19.- cruel	kind
10.	bitter	sweet	20.- wise	foolish

2. Oral Practice

restaurant (expensive/cheap)   train (long/short)   railroad (narrow/wide)

man (rich/poor)   lake (deep/shallow)   sky (clear/dark)

man (kind/cruel)   Seat belt (safe/dangerous)   scientist (wise/foolish)

3. Practice

Describe the picture using the adjective under it. Then write its opposite in the negative sentence.

Carlos
poor

He is poor.
Carlos is poor.
He is not a rich man.

room
dark

It is dark.
The room is dark.
This is not a _____ room.

Car
big

This is a _____.
This car is _____.
This is not a _____.

feather
light

This is a feather.
It is light.
It isn't a _____ feather.

Ted
short

He is _____.
Ted is _____.
He is not a _____.

horse
fast

This is a _____.
The horse is _____.
It is not a _____.

Homework: Write sentences to describe nouns using opposite adjectives.

Lesson 97

AT HOME

1 Match
Match the opposite adjectives. Write the number on the line.

___ sweet	1. empty	___ late	11. long
___ wrong	2. deep	___ false	12. polite
___ beautiful	3. cheap	___ impolite	13. true
___ dangerous	4. right	___ wide	14. thin
___ difficult	5. clear	___ short	15. early
___ dark	6. ugly	___ calm	16. narrow
___ poor	7. rich	___ foolish	17. angry
___ full	8. easy	___ fat	18. in
___ expensive	9. safe	___ out	19. cruel
___ shallow	10. bitter	___ kind	20. wise

4 Answer
Answer the statements.

1. A person that is not fat is
_____

2. A small stream is usually
_____

3. The big oceans are
_____

4. A person with good manners is
_____

5. If a statement is not good, it is
_____

6. If the test is not difficult, it is
_____

7. If the path is not narrow, it is
_____

> **Isaiah 26 : 7**
> Honesty is the path **good** people follow. They follow the path that is **straight** and **true**. And God, you make that way **smooth** and **easy** to follow.

2 Describe
Describe the objects.

_____

_____

_____

_____

_____

3 Write
Describe the nouns using the adjectives in parentheses. Make the firs sentence affirmative and the second sentence negative.

restaurant
(expensive/cheap) _____

train
(safe/dangerous) _____

man
(rich, poor) _____

sky
(clear/dark) _____

Lesson 98

Let's talk about...

Colors

Work in pairs. Ask a partner.

- How many colors do you know in English?
- What is your favorite color?
- Why do you like this particular color?
- What color of clothing do you usually wear?
- What color are your school objects?
- What color is your house?
- Do you think colors can affect your mood?

Talking about Favorites

- 1. Ask your partner about his/her favorite color.
- 2. Choose a color and list all the things you can that are of that color.
- 3. Describe your partner's/classmate's school objects. Use as many colors as you know.

Opposite Adjectives

- Look around the classroom, use the opposites list to describe objects around it.
- Use the opposite adjectives list to describe your belongings.. e.g. car, house, school objects.
- Choose 5 adjectives that best describe you.
- Describe yourself to the class.

Projects

- Pretend you are selling a certain product. Choose what you want to sell and describe it to your classmates as you show them the product. Remember you have to try to convince them to buy your product.

- Pretend you are an inventor and have a great new invention. (use your imagination and creativity to present an original invention). Show your invention to the class and describe it as much as possible. Use adjectives from the list.

Daniel and his Friends

98.1 Reference to Daniel 1:4-20

The King of Babylon wants only *healthy* and *strong* boys who do not have any bruises, scars, or anything wrong with their bodies. He gives the *young* men a certain amount of food and wine every day. He wants them to be trained for *three* years to become servants of the kingdom.

Among those *young* men are Daniel and his friends. Daniel does not want to eat the king's rich food and wine because it would make him *unclean*. So he asks Ashpenaz, the man in charge of the officials, to give them permission not to eat the king's food and wine. He is *kind* to Daniel and his friends but he is *afraid* of the king. He said, "If you don't eat this food, you will begin to look *weak* and *sick,* the king will see this, and he might cut off my head."

Then Daniel asks him to please test them for *ten* days not giving them anything but fresh vegetables to eat and water to drink. "Then after *ten* days, compare us with the other *young* men who eat the king's food. See for yourself who looks healthier, and then decide how you want to treat us." he said.

After *ten* days, Daniel and his friends looked healthier than all the *young* men who ate the king's food. God gave these *four young* men the wisdom and ability to learn many different kinds of writing and science. Daniel could also understand all kinds of visions and dreams.

At the end, these four young men became the king's servants because They were *ten* times better than all the magicians and *wise* men in his kingdom.

Circle the adjectives in the story.

Answer

1.- What words describe Daniel and his friends?

2.- What kind of food do they receive from the king?

3.- Who is the guard in charge of Daniel and his friends?

4.- What kind of food do they eat for 10 days?

5.- How do Daniel and his friends look after the 10 days?

Lesson 99

AT HOME

1 Talk about each of the illustrations about Daniel and his friends.

Ashpenah/Daniel and his friends

_____
_____
_____
_____
_____
_____
_____
_____
_____
_____

2 Write the number to indicate the correct order of the events in the story.

_____ a) Daniel asks Ashpenaz to give them permission not to eat the king's food and wine.

_____ b) Daniel does not want to eat the king's food and wine.

_____ c) Daniel and his friends do not eat the king's food for ten days.

_____ d) Ashpenaz is afraid not to feed Daniel and his friends with the king's food.

_____ e) God gave these young men wisdom and ability to learn many different kinds of writing and science.

_____ f) These four young men become the king's servants.

_____ g) After ten days, they look healthier and stronger than all the young men who eat the king's food.

_____ h) The king wants only healthy boys to serve in his palace.

3 Write the letter T (true) or F (false) on the line provided next to each statement.

_____ 1.- The four young men are taken to Babylon.

_____ 2. Ashpenaz is the king of Babylon.

_____ 3. The king wants only healthy boys to serve in his palace.

_____ 4. Daniel wants to eat the king's food and wine.

_____ 5. Daniel and his friends do not eat the king's food for ten days.

_____ 6. The king wants to train the young men for ten years.

_____ 7. Daniel and his friends eat only vegetables and drink water for ten days.

_____ 8. Ashpenaz does not help Daniel and his friends.

_____ 9. Ashpenaz is not afraid to disobey the king.

_____ 10. After ten days, the young men look healthier and stronger than all the other young men.

Lesson 100

PREPOSITIONS OF PLACE 1

A preposition of place is used to refer to the place where something or someone is located.

- Where's the dog?
The dog is among the boxes.

Psalms 109:30
I give thanks to the LORD.
I praise him **in front of** everyone.

Psalms 76:1
People **in** Judah know God.
People **in** Israel respect his name.

John 13 : 23
One of the followers was **next to** Jesus and was leaning close to him. This was the one Jesus loved very much.

WHERE ?
Where is one of the words used for asking. It asks in what place or position something or someone is.

1 Where's...?

• Where's the man?
He's **between** the desk and the chair.

• Where's the dog?
It's **in front of** the girl.

• Where's the boy?
He's **next to** the tree.

• Where's the small insect?
It's **on** the white mug.

Practice locating objects around the classroom. Use adjectives to describe them.

a. The cat is...

behind the box   in front of the box   by / next to the box

in the box   between the brown boxes.

b. Where is...?

over the box   on the brown table   under the table

Homework: Tell where the objects are using prepositions of place.

2 Oral Practice

a. Work in pairs. Ask your classmates the location of different objects in the classroom.
e.g. Where's the desk?

b. Work in pairs. Ask your classmate to tell the locations of the objects in each room.

1.   2.   3.

Homework: Write about the location of the objects in each room. Then share with your classmates.

Lesson 101

PREPOSITIONS OF PLACE II

at

It is used to discuss a certain point or place.

- at the corner
- at the bus stop
- at home
- at the entrance
- at the front desk

Peter at school

Peter at the cinema

Peter at home

Peter at the bus stop

on

Used to refer to a surface of something.

- on the table
- on the menu
- on the wall
- on a page
- on the ceiling

picture on the wall

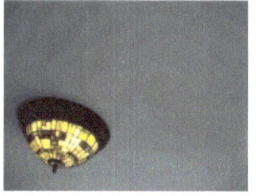
lamp on the ceiling

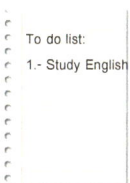
note on the page

in

It refers to a country, city, or enclosed space.

- in Paris
- in the yard
- in my pocket
- in the garden
- in the car

Peter in Paris

Adam and Eve in the garden

the parrot in its cage

2 TELL WHERE THEY ARE...

Ask your classmates where they are. Use the correct preposition of place to answer.

Peter / the zoo

Children / classroom

food / menu

Peter / New York

ball / bench

the man / at work

plant / ceiling

tools / shed

Homework: Write about the location of the objects and the people in the pictures.

AT HOME

Where are the objects?

Where is the fork?
a) It's in the glass.
b) It's near the glass.
c) It's on the glass.

Where is the ball?
a) It's in the box.
b) It's in front of the box.
c) It's on the box.

Where is the ball?
a) It's on the box.
b) It's under the box.
c) It's behind the box.

Where are the eggs?
a) They are near the nest.
b) They are in the nest.
c) They are on the nest.

Where is the ball?
a) It's under the sofa.
b) It's near the sofa.
c) It's on the sofa.

Where is the dog?
a) It's far from the doghouse.
b) It's in the doghouse.
c) It's on the doghouse.

Where is the turtle?
a) It's in the basket.
b) It's next to the basket.
c) It's behind the basket.

Where is the bird?
a) It's in the nest.
b) It's next to the nest.
c) It's in front of the nest.

Where is the t.v.?
a) It's in the trash can.
b) It's near the trash can.
c) It's on the trashcan.

Where is the straw?
a) It's in the glass.
b) It's in front of the glass.
c) It's on the glass.

Where is the ball?
a) It's over the bear.
b) It's under the bear.
c) It's behind he bear.

Where is the parrot?
a) It's in the cage.
b) It's behind the cage.
c) It's next to the cage.

Where is the tree?
a) It's in front of the house.
b) It's behind the house.
c) It's next to the house.

Where is the house?
a) It's between the trees.
b) It's far from the trees.
c) It's behind the trees.

Where is the ball?
a) It's under the stool.
b) It's near the stool.
c) It's on the stool.

Where is the man?
a) He's next to the dog.
b) He's far from the dog.
c) He's near the dog.

Where is the frog?
a) It's among the flowers.
b) It's far from the flowers.
c) It's next to the flowers.

Where is the snail?
a) It's between the bushes.
b) It's among the bushes
c) It's behind the bushes.

Where is the cake?
a) It's under the table.
b) It's near the table.
c) It's on the table.

Where is the bone?
a) It's far from the dog.
b) It's next to the dog.
c) It's behind the dog.

Homework: Write questions about the location of objects. Then answer them and share with the class.

Lesson **103**

AT HOME

WRITING

1 Answer the questions. Tell where the people and objects are. Give complete answers.

Where's the man?
_____

Where's the dog?
_____

Where's the boy?
_____

Where's the bug?
_____

Where's the cat?
_____

Where's the boy?
_____

Where's Peter?
_____

2 Tell where the objects are. Write the missing preposition of place on the line provided.

The lamp is_____the plant,_____the sofa.
The sofa is_____the living room,_____the fireplace and the plant.
The painting is_____the sofa,_____from the cat.
The plant is_____the lamp,_____the sofa.
The cat is_____the floor,_____the fireplace.

The coffee table is_____the carpet,_____the sofa.
The armchair is_____the sofa,_____from the curtains.
The carpet is_____the floor,_____the sofa.
The lamp is_____the fish tank_____the curtains.
The fish tank is_____the coffee table_____from the armchair.

The books are_____the bookshelf,_____the radio.
The bed is_____the curtains_____from the books.
The radio is _____the bookshelf,_____the books and the curtains.
The hanger is_____the bed,_____the cell phone.
The cell phone is _____the soccer ball,_____from the lamp.

Homework: Write your own sentences telling where the objects in each room are.

114

Singular and Plural Nouns

Lesson 104

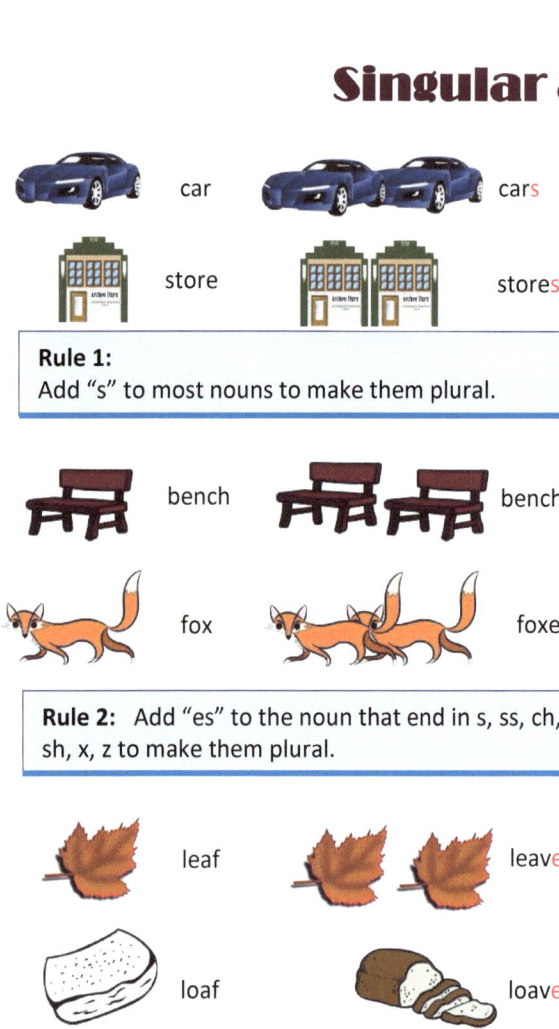

A Noun is a person, place, animal, thing or idea.

Rule 1: Add "s" to most nouns to make them plural.

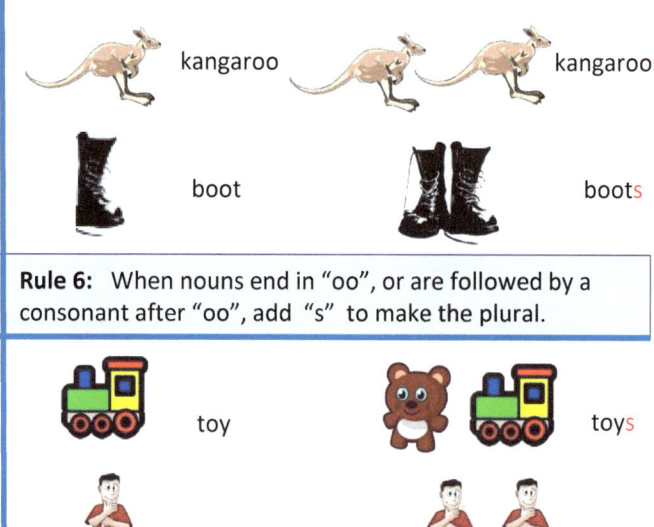

Rule 2: Add "es" to the noun that end in s, ss, ch, sh, x, z to make them plural.

Rule 6: When nouns end in "oo", or are followed by a consonant after "oo", add "s" to make the plural.

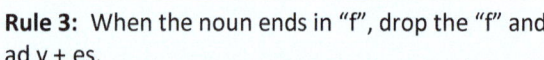

Rule 3: When the noun ends in "f", drop the "f" and ad v + es.

Rule 7: Add "s" when the nouns end in a vowel and "y".

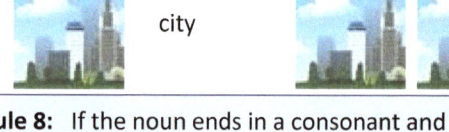

Rule 4: When the noun ends in "fe", drop the "fe" and add "v + es". Exception to the rule: chef- chefs

Rule 8: If the noun ends in a consonant and "y", change the "y" to "i" and add "es".

Practice:
Write the plural form of the nouns.

This is a sharp knife.	These	knives	are sharp.
That is a big potato.	_____	_____	are big.
That is a nice toy.	_____	_____	are nice.
This is a wild fox.	_____	_____	are wild.
That is an orange leaf.	_____	_____	are orange.
That is a pretty bench.	_____	_____	are pretty.
This is a new car.	_____	_____	are new.

Rule 5: Add "es" to nouns ending in "o". Exception to the rule: piano

AT HOME

Lesson 105

1 Complete
Complete the statements with the words from the box. You can use each preposition more than once.

behind	in front of	by	in	next to
under	among	at	over	on	between

1. The money is _____ the wallet.
2. The boys are playing _____ their room.
3. The dog is sleeping _____ the chair.
4. There is a coffee shop _____ of my house.
5. There are two white roses _____ the tulips.
6. My best friend lives _____ the river.
7. My cat plays in the area _____ the house.
8. The bird flies _____ the roof of the house.
9. Please sit _____ me during the English class.
10. I have to be early _____ home today.
11. There are new good options _____ the menu.
12. My family picture is _____ the wall.
13. I am sorry to drop the paper. It´s _____ the floor.
14. There is a parrot _____ those birds.
15. The girls like to sit _____ the yard.
16. Come! I found a fresh place to sit _____ a tall tree.
17. My son likes to fly his kite _____ the houses.
18. Where is your father? Is he _____ the car?

2 Word Search
Find and circle 14 plural nouns hidden. Then write them on the lines provided.

```
a s t u d e n t s c e y e s
n e t h f p c i e u u r u r
i n s u r a l e a r s a c a
m t h n o p o c i t i e s p
a l o g g e t t a d e t e
l b e d s r k r e i s e s n
s d r e s s e s g n b o y s
c o m p u t e r s s t o e s
```

1. _____   8. _____
2. _____   9. _____
3. _____   10. _____
4. _____   11. _____
5. _____   12. _____
6. _____   13. _____
7. _____   14. _____

3 Write the plural form of the following nouns on the line provided.

1. boy _____
2. toy _____
3. box _____
4. tree _____
5. house _____
6. chicken _____
7. fence _____
8. truck _____
9. city _____
10. store _____
11. bench _____
12. leaf _____
13. zoo _____
14. fox _____
15. fence _____
16. knife _____
17. wife _____
18. dime _____

4 Write sentences with the plural nouns on exercise 2.

1.- _____
2.- _____
3.- _____
4.- _____
5.- _____
6.- _____

5 Circle the correct plural form for each noun in the oval.

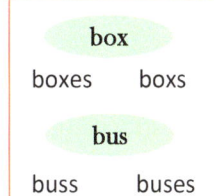

- **box**: boxes / boxs
- **bus**: buss / buses
- **tax**: taxs / taxes
- **rabbit**: rabbites / rabbits
- **penny**: pennys / pennies
- **fox**: foxs / foxes
- **bag**: bages / bags
- **ruby**: rubies / rubys

116

The Creation of the World

1 On the first day "God said, Let there be light";  and there was light.
Genesis 1:3

2 On the second day God divided the waters below from the waters above,  and created heaven.

3 On the third day God commanded the waters to be gathered together into one place,  and he made the dry land appear.

On the earth He created all the grasses, plants, and trees.

4 On the fourth day God made the sun, the moon, and the stars.

5 On the fifth day God created all the living creatures that live in the waters,  and also all of the birds of the air.

6 On the sixth day God made all the creatures, which live on land:  the beasts, and the cattle, and the creeping things.

Also on the sixth day, God made a man and a woman.  God created them in His own image.

7

God saw everything that He had made, and indeed it was very good.
Genesis 1:31

On the seventh day, God was finished with all His work, and He rested.

Lesson 107

Let's talk about ...
The Creation of the World

Reference to Genesis 1: 1-28

The earth was empty. There was nothing on the earth. Darkness covered the ocean, and God's Spirit moved over the water.

1st Day - Light
Then God says, "Let there be light!" And light begins to shine. God names the light "day," and the darkness "night."

2nd Day - Sky
Then God says, "Let there be a space to separate the water into two parts!" . Some of the water is above it, and some of the water is below it.

3rd Day - Land and Plants
Then God says, "Let the water under the sky be gathered together so that the dry land will appear." Then God creates grass, plants, and fruit trees with fruit in them.

4th Day - Sun, Moon, and Stars
Then God says, "Let there be lights in the sky. These lights will separate the days from the nights. They will be in the sky to shine light on the earth." He also creates the stars. God puts them in the sky to rule over the day and over the night.

5th Day - Fish and Birds
Then God says, "Let the water be filled with many living things, and let there be birds to fly in the air over the earth." So God creates the animals in the sea and every kind of bird that flies in the air.

6th Day - Land Animals and People
Then God says, "Let there be animals on land. He creates the wild animals, the tame animals, and all the small crawling things. Then, God created humans in his own image and blessed them.

7th Day - God rests

Circle : plural nouns in blue, prepositions of place in red, adjectives with a different color.

ORDINAL NUMBERS - 1ST TO 20TH

| 1st | 2nd | 3rd | 4th | 5th | 6th | 7th | 8th | 9th | 10th |
| 11th | 12th | 13th | 14th | 15th | 16th | 17th | 18th | 19th | 20th |

1st	**first**	6th	**sixth**	11th	**eleventh**	16th	**sixteenth**
2nd	**second**	7th	**seventh**	12th	**twelfth**	17th	**seventeenth**
3rd	**third**	8th	**eighth**	13th	**thirteenth**	18th	**eighteenth**
4th	**fourth**	9th	**ninth**	14th	**fourteenth**	19th	**nineteenth**
5th	**fifth**	10th	**tenth**	15th	**fifteenth**	20th	**twentieth**

Answer:

1. What ordinal numbers do you find in the article about the creation of the world?
   1st, 2nd, 3rd, 4th, 5th, 6th, 7th. (each of the days of the creation.)
2. Who of your classmates is the first student in the attendance list?
   Answers may vary
3. Who is the person sitting in the third place in your line?

4. Tell some plural nouns that you found in the article of the creation of the world.
   Animals, lights, things, humans, stars

Ephesians 6:2
The command says, "You must respect your father and mother." This is the **first** command that has a promise with it.

Lesson 108

AT HOME

1 Write the plural nouns you find in the article of the creation of the world.

1. _____ 3. _____ 5. _____ 7. _____
2. _____ 4. _____ 6. _____ 8. _____

2 Tell what God created every day. Use complete sentences.

The **1st** day: _____ The **4th** day: _____

The **2nd** day: _____ The **5th** day: _____

The **3rd** day: _____ The **6th** day: _____

3 Write the word for each ordinal number.

1 st _____   6 th _____   11 th _____   16 th _____
2 nd _____   7 th _____   12 th _____   17 th _____
3 rd _____   8 th _____   13 th _____   18 th _____
4 th _____   9 th _____   14 th _____   19 th _____
5 th _____   10 th _____ 15 th _____   20 th _____

4 Circle the ordinal numbers you find.

> Reference to Matthew 22 :33-39
>
> People were amazed at Jesus' teaching. One of the Pharisees, an expert in the Law of Moses, asked Jesus a question to test him. He said, "Teacher, which command in the law is the most important?" Jesus answered, "Love the Lord your God with all your heart, all your soul, and all your mind."
>
> This is the **first** and most important command. And the **second** command is like the **first**: 'Love your neighbor the same as you love yourself.'

Answer:

1. Who was teaching?
_____
2. Who asked Jesus a question?
_____
3. Which is the first command in the law of God?
_____
4. Which is the second command?
_____

5 Use the calendar to answer the questions.

FEBRUARY

Sun.	Mon.	Tues	Wed.	Thurs	Fri.	Sat.
					1	2
3	4	5	6	7	8	9
10	11	12	13	14	15	16
17	18	19	20	21	22	23
24	25	26	27	28		

(Note: calendar shows 1–28 with days as: Sun=1, Mon=2, Tues=3, Wed=4, Thurs=5, Fri=6, Sat=7, then 8-14, 15-21, 22-28)

1. What place does the month February have in the calendar? _____

2. What is the sixth month of the year? _____

3. What is the 10th month of the year? _____

4. What is the first day of February? _____

5. What is the third day of the month of February? _____

6. What is the 18th day of the month? _____

UNIT 9 SUMMARY

SHAPES

circle	hexagon
oval	pentagon
star	diamond
cross	triangle
arrow	rectangle
square	parallelogram
heart	octagon

- What shape is this?
  This is a _____.

- What shape is that?
  That is a _____.

COLORS

red	dark green
brown	light green
yellow	dark blue
maroon	light blue
peach	light gray
pink	dark brown
purple	light brown
white	dusty pink
black	soft pink
gray	light purple
aqua	orange
green	

- What color is the cap?
  The cap is blue.

PREPOSITIONS OF PLACE

behind:	The boy is hiding behind the sofa.
in front of:	The student is in front of the desk.
by:	We will camp by the lake tomorrow.
next to:	He lives next to the gas station.
between:	The boy is between his two sisters.
over:	The plane flies over the mountain.
under:	The cat is under the chair.
among:	The butterfly is among the flowers.
at:	I am at home on Sundays afternoon.
in:	The markers are in the pencil case.
on:	The book is on the table.

OPPOSITE ADJECTIVES I

1. high	low	11. strong	weak
2. wet	dry	12. pretty	ugly
3. near	far	13. big	small
4. quiet	loud	14. fast	slow
5. cold	hot	15. young	old
6. clean	dirty	16. new	old
7. good	bad	17. happy	sad
8. left	right	18. enormous	tiny
9. dark	light	19. tall	short
10. heavy	light	20. clever	silly

OPPOSITE ADJECTIVES II

1. empty	full	11. long	short
2. deep	shallow	12. polite	impolite
3. cheap	expensive	13. true	false
4. right	wrong	14. thin	fat
5. clear	dark	15. early	late
6. ugly	beautiful	16. narrow	wide
7. rich	poor	17. angry	calm
8. easy	difficult	18. in	out
9. safe	dangerous	19. cruel	kind
10. bitter	sweet	20. wise	foolish

PLURAL NOUNS

Rule 1: add "s" to most nouns.   tree – trees

Rule 2: add "es" to nouns that end in: s, ss, ch, sh, x, z
e.g. church – churches

Rule 3: when the nouns end if "f", drop it and add "v+es"
e.g. loaf – loaves

Rule 4: when the noun ends in "fe", drop the "fe" and add "v" + "es".   eg. wife – wives

Rule 5: add "es" to nouns ending in "o".   hero – heroes

Rule 6: add "s" to nouns ending in "oo".   zoo – zoos

Rule 7: add "s" to nouns ending in a vowel + "y".   e.g. valley – valleys

Rule 8: when the nouns end in a consonant and "y", change the "y" to "i" and add "es".   e.g. candy - candies

Location of objects

Singular:
Where is the bug?
(Where's the bug?)

Plural:
Where are the bugs?

ORDINAL NUMBERS

1st	first	11th	eleventh
2nd	second	12th	twelfth
3rd	third	13th	thirteenth
4th	fourth	14th	fourteenth
5th	fifth	15th	fifteenth
6th	sixth	16th	sixteenth
7th	seventh	17th	seventeenth
8th	eighth	18th	eighteenth
9th	ninth	19th	nineteenth
10th	tenth	20th	twentieth

GRAMMAR

Adjectives are used in 2 ways

That bug is small.
(noun + verb to be + adjective)

That is a small bug.

UNIT 10

ESOL CHILDREN - GUATEMALA

INTRODUCTION

In this unit, you will learn new vocabulary about the family and will be able to talk about your family using the different tenses of the verb to be.

You will also learn about jobs and occupations and be able to read some stories about disciples and their jobs.
You will also be able to talk about people's jobs.

There are also different Bible scriptures and stories related to each of the topics.

OBJECTIVES

- Learn vocabulary about the family.
- Practice the verb to be in affirmative, negative e interrogative forms.
- Talk about your family.
- Learn vocabulary about Jobs and occupations.
- Talk and read about different jobs and occupations.
- Practice reading Bible scriptures about the different topics.

Feelings and Emotions

Lesson 109

1 Vocabulary 🎧 109.1

 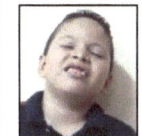  

weak   sick   sleepy   angry

jealous   sad   upset   mad

2 How are you today?

Finish the expressions using each adjective.

Today, I am _____.
I'm very _____ today.

tired   sick   sad

How is he today?

Today, he is _____.
He's very _____ today.

angry   hot   sleepy

How are they today?

Today, they are _____.
They're very _____ today.

hungry   thirsty   hot

3 Reading Practice

1. The children are happy.
2. The man is hungry.
3. My friend is cold.
4. The boys are thirsty.
5. The boy is sick.
6. The girl is very tired.
7. They are very hot.
8. Carmen is sleepy.
9. Rolando is in love.
10. Rosa is angry.

4 Verb to Be

I am Marcos.
You are my friend.
We are friends.
They are my parents.
He is a student.
She is a teacher.
It is my pet.

I	am
You / We / They	are
He / She / It	is

🎧 109.5 God sends Jonah to Nineveh

The LORD tells Jonah to give the city of Nineveh a message "After 40 days Nineveh will be destroyed". When they hear the message, they believe in God and show him that they are *sad* about their sins. They decide to change and stop doing bad things.

God sees what the people do and he does not punish the people. Jonah is not *happy* about it. Jonah is *angry*. God asks Jonah, "Do you think it is right for you to be *angry*?"

Jonah sits to see the city. The Lord makes a gourd plant grow quickly over Jonah. This makes a cool place for Jonah to sit. He is very *happy* because of the plant but the next morning God sends a worm to eat the plant. The sun becomes very hot on Jonah's head, and he becomes very *weak*. Jonah is very *angry* about this. The Lord says to Jonah, "Why are you *sad* because the plant died? If you can get *upset* over a plant, surely I can feel sorry for a big city like Nineveh."

                      Reference to Jonah 3-4

Answer T (True) or F (False).

1. ____ Jonah gives Nineveh a message of destruction.
2. ____ The people do not listen to the message.
3. ____ God destroys the city of Nineveh.
4. ____ Jonah is angry because God forgave the people.
5. ____ Jonah is happy when the plant grows over his head.

Chelsea is angry.
She is an angry girl.

Mary and Indira are happy.
They are happy women.

Ramiro is sad.
He is a sad boy.

Pedro is mad.
He is mad.

Subject Pronoun + verb to be + feeling

Lesson 110

At Home

1 Unscramble
Unscramble the words to make sentences. Then, write them on the line.

1. am/I/happy/today
_____
2. mother/my/tired/very/is/today
_____
3. hungry/are/children/the
_____
4. today/sick/friend/my/is
_____
5. thirsty/are/very/they
_____

2 Unscramble
Unscramble the words. Write the words on the lines.

1. ygarn _____
2. dtrie _____
3. yhs _____
4. peyesl _____
5. ghnuyr _____
6. locd _____
7. yhpap _____
8. amd _____
9. das _____
10. toh _____
11. ksic _____
12. ystihrt _____

3 word search
Find the 12 words hidden. Write the words on the lines provided.

```
a n g r y a u p s e t h
m i x h a c o l d d h a
a f t u t b l t i m i p
d v l n s l e e p y r p
o i n g e d c k t e s y
u u f r t i r e d t t p
s s h y s c l s o d y o
s a d i l t y x s i c k
```

_____
_____
_____
_____
_____
_____
_____
_____
_____
_____
_____
_____

4 Grammar
Write the correct form of the verb To Be.

1. He _____ a good man.
2. The boy _____ sick.
3. They _____ sad.
4. The girl _____ sleepy.
5. Sandra _____ tired.
6. I _____ hungry.
7. We _____ hot.
8. Jorge and I _____ sad.
9. They _____ nice.
10. He _____ my friend.
11. The man _____ mad.
12. They _____ happy.
13. Marta _____ cold.
14. It _____ hot today.
15. The dog _____ sad.
16. It _____ sick.
17. We _____ thirsty.
18. They _____ angry.
19. Sam _____ upset.
20. The boys _____ sad.

5 Write
Write sentences with the words.

1. tired
_____
2. sleepy
_____
3. hungry
_____
4. sick
_____
5. thirsty
_____
6. cold
_____
7. happy
_____
8. sad
_____
9. angry
_____

6 Write
Write about the people in the pictures.

_____
_____
_____
_____

_____
_____
_____
_____

123

Lesson 111

The Family

1 🎧 Vocabulary

1. the family	16. uncle
2. father	17. cousin
3. dad	18. nephew
4. mother	19. niece
5. mom	20. grandparents
6. the children	21. grandfather
7. child	22. grandmother
8. son	23. grandchildren
9. daughter	24. granddaughter
10. brother	25. grandson
11. sister	26. baby
12. siblings	27. the twins
13. wife	28. the triplets
14. husband	29. the only son
15. aunt	30. relatives

She's Susan.
She's my mother.
She's upset.

They're Mary and Indira.
They're friends.
They're happy.
They're ESOL students.

He's Ramiro.
He's my brother-in-law.
He's sad.

He's Carlos.
Carlos is my grandfather.
He's disgusted.

We're a family.
We're from Mexico.
We're happy.

She's my mother-in-law.
She's my friend.
She's angry.

2 Practice with your classmates
Use the verb to be to talk about them.

Jorge — father Susana — daughter Maria — mother Karla — aunt Pablo — uncle

 Ben, John, Sara — cousins    Martha — grandmother

Personal Pronouns
I	We	He	It
You	They	She	

3 Reading Practice

1. The family's in the house.
2. My father's at home.
3. My sister is sad.
4. The boys are my brothers.
5. The boy's my nephew.
6. Mary is a happy girl.
7. They're my parents.
8. My sister's a good nurse.
9. My uncle's a good man.
10. They're my cousins.
11. My aunt Susan is very happy.
12. My beautiful mother is cold.
13. We're a beautiful family.
14. Carlos is far from school.
15. Carmen's my aunt.
16. They're my relatives.
17. My mother is angry.
18. My brother is smart.

To Be - Contractions
I am Marcos.	I'm
You are my friend.	You're
We are friends.	We're
They are my parents.	They're
He is a student.	He's
She is a teacher.	She's
It is my pet.	It's

Pronoun + verb to be + noun

Homework: Study the vocabulary. Practice writing sentences using the vocabulary.

At Home

Lesson 112

1 Unscramble
Unscramble the letters in the box.
Write the correct word on the line provided

1.- dreldichnangr _____
2.- ybab _____
3.- botrhre _____
4.- redhagut _____
5.- hretafndrga _____
6.- tsniw _____
7.- sslbgnii _____
8.- nluce _____
9.- hewnep _____
10. yalfmi _____

2 Describe
Write about people in your family.
Describe some of your relatives. Write the word for each in the box.

3 Writing
Write sentences with the words from the box.

1.- sister-in-law _____
2.- grandson _____
3.- niece _____
4.- aunt _____
5.- child _____
6.- grandmother _____
7.- father _____
8.- grandchildren _____
9.- wife _____
10.- cousin _____

4 Verb to Be
Write the correct form of the verb to be in the present tense provided.

1. My brother _____ thirsty.
2. They _____ my parents.
3. My mother _____ at home.
4. Julia and Roberto _____ my cousins.
5. My grandparents _____ in the house.
6. My sister _____ in the car.
7. They _____ my siblings.
8. The boy _____ my little brother.
9. My friend Joe _____ an only son.
10. My cousin _____ an adopted child.
11. My relatives _____ in my sister's house.
12. Juan _____ her stepfather.

Homework: Practice writing the new words.

125

Lesson 113

Let's talk about ...

The Family

> **Exodus 20:12**
> "You must honor and respect your **father** and your **mother**. Do this so that you will have a full life in the land that the LORD your God gives you."

How can we honor our father and mother?
_____

God commands us to honor our parents. What will happen to us if we obey this commandment?
_____

> **Reference to Joshua 24:15**
> "But maybe you don't want to serve the LORD. Today you must decide who you will serve. Will you serve the gods that your ancestors? Or will you serve the gods who lived in this land? You must choose for yourselves. But as for me and my family, we will serve the LORD."

Whom must we serve?
_____

How can you serve the Lord in your family?
_____

> **Proverbs 1:8**
> My son, listen to your father when he corrects you, and don't ignore what your mother teaches you.
>
> **Proverbs 1:9**
> What you learn from your parents will bring you honor and respect, like a crown or a gold medal

Is it easy to receive correction?
_____

As a child, what do you do when your parents correct you?

If you are a parent, do you correct your children?
_____

Homework: Talk about the people in your family.

> **Proverbs 22:6**
> Teach children in a way they should go, and even when they are old, they will not leave the right path.

Why is it important to teach young children about God?
_____

> **1 Timothy 5:7-8**
> Tell the believers there to take care of their **family** so that no one can say they are doing wrong.
> Everyone should take care of all their own people. Most importantly, they should take care of their own **family**. If they do not do that, then they do not accept what we believe. They are worse than someone who does not even believe in God.

How can we take care of our family?

The Family Tree

Talk about your family. Make a chart with pictures of people in your family.

Work in pairs. Ask each other the following questions.

1. Is your family big or small?
2. Do you have brothers and sisters?
3. What's you mother's name?
4. Do you have children?
5. Where is your father from?

Lesson 114

JOBS AND OCCUPATIONS I

1 🎧 114.1 VOCABULARY

1. doctor	16. carpenter
2. police officer	17. cashier
3. firefighter	18. construction worker
4. mail carrier	19. dentist
5. nurse	20. engineer
6. bus driver	21. farmer
7. pilot	22. plumber
8. teacher	23. reporter
9. waiter	24. secretary
10. barber	25. security guard
11. student	26. soldier
12. cook	27. veterinarian
13. actor	28. waitress
14. actress	29. eye doctor
15. astronaut	30. dancer

Kathy is my mother in law.
She's not a secretary.
She's a reporter.
She works in Hope Productions.

Pedro is my cousin.
He's not a farmer.
He's a veterinarian.
He works at the Pet Hospital.

Maria and Carla are twins.
They're not dancers.
They're students.

My friend Tomas is not a waiter.
He's a security guard.
He works in a security company.

 Hi! My name is Allan Gonzales. I'm 9 years old. I'm not a teacher. I'm a student. Who are you?

Hi! I'm Estuardo Rodriguez. I'm not a cook. I'm a chef. I work in a famous restaurant. I'm from Guatemala.

2 PRACTICE WITH A PARTNER

1. Who are you?
   Are you a soldier?
   -No. I am not.
   Are you a vet?
   -Yes. I am a vet.

   ✗ soldier   ✗ bus driver
   ✓ veterinarian ✓ taxi driver

   ✗ eye doctor   ✗ plumber
   ✓ astronaut   ✓ mail carrier

2. Who is she?
   Is she a waitress?
   -No. She isn't.
   Is she an actress?
   -Yes. She is an actress.

   ✗ waitress ✗ gardener   ✗ cashier ✗ secretary
   ✓ actress   ✓ firefighter ✓ dancer   ✓ nurse

3. Who are they?
   Are they engineers?
   -No. They aren't.
   Are they actors?
   -Yes. They are actors.

   ✗ dancers   ✗ cooks
   ✓ soldiers   ✓ chefs

   ✗ students   ✗ veterinarians
   ✓ barbers   ✓ eye doctors

   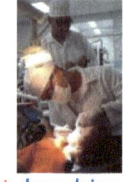

✗ engineers ✗ lawyers ✗ actors   ✗ bus drivers
✓ actors   ✓ bakers   ✓ teachers ✓ dentists

Grammar

Affirmative:	I am a student.
Negative:	I am not a student.
Interrogative:	Am I a student?
Affirmative:	You are a nurse.
Negative:	You are not a nurse.
Interrogative:	Are you a nurse?
Affirmative:	We are teachers.
Negative:	We are not teachers.
Interrogative:	Are we teachers?
Affirmative:	They are pilots.
Negative:	They are not pilots.
Interrogative:	Are they pilots?
Affirmative:	He is a student.
Negative:	He is not a student.
Interrogative:	Is he a student?
Affirmative:	She is a teacher.
Negative:	She is not a teacher.
Interrogative:	Is she a teacher?

At Home

Lesson **115**

1 Unscramble
Unscramble the words.
Write the answer on the line provided.

1. frihgtreefi _____
2. erbarb _____
3. atnuasrot _____
4. npreatecr _____
5. itdnest _____
6. neregnie _____
7. mrafre _____
8. toreprer _____
9. iserdlo _____
10. tirsesaw _____

2 Jobs and Occupations
Write the correct occupation on the line provided.

secretary   teacher   veterinarian   plumber   farmer
bus driver   soldier   construction worker   eye doctor   dentist

1. A _____ helps building houses.
2. A _____ fights in wars.
3. A _____ helps sick animals.
4. An _____ checks your eyes.
5. A _____ examines your teeth.
6. A _____ grows crops.
7. A _____ fixes sinks.
8. A _____ drive children to school.
9. A _____ teaches children how to read.
10. A _____ writes letters.

3 WRITE ABOUT THEM.

Antonio
Who is he?
He's Antonio.
Antonio is not a waiter.
He's a construction worker.
✗ waiter
✓ construction worker

Lester
Who is he?
_____
_____
_____
✗ plumber
✓ teacher

Deysi
Who is she?
_____
✗ _____
✓ _____
✗ reporter
✓ actress

Karla
Who is she?
_____
✗ _____
✓ _____
✗ veterinarian
✓ firefighter

Francis
Who is she?
_____
✗ _____
✓ _____
✗ pilot
✓ nurse

Francisco Fu
Who is he?
_____
✗ _____
✓ _____
✗ eye doctor
✓ dentist

4 VERB TO BE.
Write the correct form of the verb to be. Then, change the sentence to negative form.

1.- They _____ English teachers.
2.- We _____ reporters.
3.- I _____ a firefighter.
4.- You _____ an engineer.

1.- _____.
2.- _____.
3.- _____.
4.- _____.

128

Lesson 116

JOBS AND OCCUPATIONS II

1. Vocabulary

1. scientist
2. coach
3. politician
4. deliveryman
5. baker
6. butcher
7. surgeon
8. florist
9. archaeologist
10. mechanic
11. artist
12. athlete
13. salesperson
14. musician
15. photographer
16. electrician
17. businessman
18. architect
19. dressmaker
20. farmer
21. painter
22. hairdresser
23. gardener
24. lawyer
25. baby-sitter
26. singer
27. waiter
28. fisherman
29. mason
30. air hostess
31. taxi driver
32. barman

2. Who are they?
Practice short answers.

Who is she?
Is she a salesperson?
No, she isn't.
Is she a baker?
Yes, she is.

Who is he?
Is he a surgeon?
No, he isn't.
Is he a photographer?
Yes, he is.

Who are they?
Are they masons?
No, they aren't.
Are they painters?
Yes, they are.

Who are you?
Are you a taxi driver?
No, I'm not.
Are you a bus driver?
Yes, I am.

3. Are you a doctor?

Hi! I'm Allan. Who are you?
Are you a photographer?

Hi! I'm Javier.
No. I'm not. I'm a painter.

Practice with a partner.

| ✗ electrician | ✗ butcher | ✗ surgeon | ✗ deliveryman |
| ✓ waiter | ✓ lawyer | ✓ painter | ✓ mechanic |

4. Is she a gardener?

Hi! I'm Allan. Who is she?
Is she a gardener?

She's Rosa.
No. She isn't. She's a dressmaker.

Practice with a partner.

Rosa  Angela Mayra  Hector

| ✗ gardener | ✗ lawyer | ✗ baby-sitter | ✗ archaeologist |
| ✓ dressmaker | ✓ baker | ✓ air hostess | ✓ musician |

Grammar

Affirmative: I am a singer.
Negative: I am not a butcher.
Question: Am I an athlete?
　Yes. You are/No. You're not.

Affirmative: You are an artist.
Negative: You are not a mechanic.
Question: Are you a surgeon?
　Yes. I am/No. I'm not.

Affirmative: We are musicians.
Negative: We are not electricians.
Question: Are we photographers?
　Yes. We are/No. We're not.

Affirmative: They are archaeologists.
Negative: They are not gardeners.
Question: Are they hairdressers?
　Yes. They are/No. They're not.

Affirmative: She is an airline hostess.
Negative: She is not a dressmaker.
Question: Is she a salesperson?
　Yes. She is/No. She isn't.

Lesson 117

At Home

1 Unscramble
Unscramble the words. Write the correct answer on the line provided.

1. smasnuisneb _____
2. ssmerdakre _____
3. ssedrreaihr _____
4. naymevrlied _____
5. stargoloeicha_____
6. nosrpselase _____
7. erpagrohtoph_____
8. acinopilti _____
9. eecltrcaiin _____
10. amrefishn _____

2 Verb to Be
Write the correct occupation on the line provided.

1. A_____ makes gardens look beautiful.
2. A_____ delivers delicious pizza.
3. A_____ prepares cakes.
4. A _____ sells different kinds of meat.
5. An_____ practices sports.
6. An_____ works with electricity.
7. A_____ sings songs.
8. A_____ works with wood.
9. A_____ can change the color of your house.
10. An_____ draws and paints beautiful pictures.

3 Write
Write the question for each occupation. Answer the questions.

Antonio
Is Antonio a waiter? _____
✗ No, he isn't. _____
Is he a construction worker? _____
✓ Yes, he is. He's a construction worker. _____

✗ waiter
✓ construction worker

Manuel
_____
✗ _____
_____
✓ _____

✗ lawyer
✓ teacher

Rosa
_____
✗ _____
_____
✓ _____

✗ hairdresser
✓ dressmaker

Angel
_____
✗ _____
_____
✓ _____

✗ waitress
✓ baker

The men
_____
✗ _____
_____
✓ _____

✗ masons
✓ actors

Ana
_____
✗ _____
_____
✓ _____

✗ musician
✓ artist

4 Verb to Be
Write the correct form of the verb to be on the line. Then, change the sentence to questions.

1. Carlos _____ a mason.
2. My sister _____ an air hostess.
3. My mother and I _____ artists.
4. Pedro _____ a fisherman.

1. _____.
2. _____.
3. _____.
4. _____.

130

Lesson 118

Let's talk about...

Occupations

Colossians 3:23-24
"Whatever you do, work at it with all your heart, as working for the Lord, not for men, since you know that you will receive an inheritance from the Lord as Reward. It is the Lord Christ you are serving."

Exodus 35:35
He has given both of these men special skills to do all kinds of work. They are able to do the work of carpenters and metalworkers.

Isaiah 64:8
But now, LORD, you are our Father. We are the clay, and you are our potter. We are the work of your hands.

Ephesians 6:5-6
Slaves, obey your earthly masters with proper respect. Be as sincere as you are when you obey Christ.

Don't obey them only while you're being watched, as if you merely wanted to please people. But obey like slaves who belong to Christ, who have a deep desire to do what God wants them to do.

- How do we have to do work?
- According to the Bible what kind of worker should you be?

Hi! My name is Beyra Fernandez. I'm 29 years old. I am from Managua. I work in a Café. I am learning English in the ESOL Program.

Hi! My name is Luz Serrano. I'm from Nicaragua. I'm a Christian. I have a degree in Finances. I work in a theater. I'm married. My husband is a technician.

Hi! My name's Rosa Amalia. I'm from Honduras. I'm a Christian. I am as a dressmaker and have my own business. I'm learning English in the ESOL Program to have better job opportunities.

Hi! My name is Angela. I am a baker. I bake delicious bread and cakes. I'm very happy because I have my own bakery. I'm from San Pedro Sula, Honduras.

READ THE DIALOGUE (118.1)

Sindy: Hello Mary! How are you today?
Mary: Hi! I'm fine. How about you?
Sindy: I'm good. I got the job I told you about. I'm very happy with my new job.
Mary: Oh! Really? I am glad to hear that. Congratulations!
Sindy: Yes, thank you. I really like my job. I work as an English teacher.
Mary: That sounds great!
Sindy: Oh.. Yes, it is. It is so good to work with children.
Mary: I am very happy for you my friend.
Sindy: Thank you! I just wanted to tell you the good news. See you tomorrow at church.
Mary: Yes. Thank you my friend. See you!

Tips for a Successful Job Interview

1. Dress properly. The way you look is very important. Try to cause a good impression with a professional appearance.

2. Find out about the employer or company. It is important to know the kind of job or company you are applying for and to prepare your answers in an interview.

3. Review common and expected interview questions and prepare your answers.

4. Arrive on time. It would cause a negative impression to arrive late for the interview. Try to get to the interview at least 10 minutes before.

UNIT 10 SUMMARY

FEELINGS/EMOTIONS

weak   cold
sick   sad
sleepy   upset
angry   mad
tired   hot
shy   happy
hungry

The man is angry.
They are upset.
She is sleepy.
The boy is sad.
I am tired.
He is sick.

THE FAMILY

1. the family
2. father
3. dad
4. mother
5. mom
6. the children
7. child
8. son
9. daughter
10. brother
11. sister
12. siblings
13. wife
14. husband
15. aunt
16. uncle
17. cousin
18. nephew
19. niece
20. grandparents
21. grandfather
22. grandmother
23. grandchildren
24. granddaughter
25. grandson
26. baby
27. the twins
28. the triplets
29. the only son
30. relatives

TO BE - SHORT ANSWERS

Are you a taxi driver?
No, I'm not.
Are you a bus driver?
Yes, I am.

Is he a teacher?
No, he's not.
Is he a scientist?
Yes, he is.

Are they actors?
No, they aren't.
Are they mail carriers?
Yes, they are.

TO BE - CONTRACTIONS

I'm — I am Marcos.
You're — You are my friend.
We're — We are friends.
They're — They are my parents.
He's — He is a student.
She's — She is a teacher.
It's — It is my pet.

SUBJECT PRONOUNS

I — I am Marcos.

You / We / They
You are my friend.
We are friends.
They are my parents.

He / She / It
He is a student.
She is a teacher.
It is my pet.

VERB TO BE

Aff.: I am a teacher.
Neg.: I am not a teacher.
Int.: Am I a teacher?

Aff.: She is a teacher.
Neg.: She is not a teacher.
Int.: Is she a teacher?

Aff.: You are teachers.
Neg.: You are not teachers.
Int.: Are you teachers?

JOBS AND OCCUPATIONS I

1. doctor
2. police officer
3. firefighter
4. mail carrier
5. nurse
6. bus driver
7. pilot
8. teacher
9. waiter
10. barber
11. student
12. cook
13. actor
14. actress
15. astronaut
16. carpenter
17. cashier
18. construction worker
19. dentist
20. engineer
21. farmer
22. plumber
23. reporter
24. secretary
25. security guard
26. soldier
27. veterinarian
28. waitress
29. eye doctor
30. dancer

JOBS AND OCCUPATIONS II

1. scientist
2. couch
3. politician
4. deliveryman
5. baker
6. butcher
7. surgeon
8. florist
9. archaeologist
10. mechanic
11. artist
12. athlete
13. salesperson
14. musician
15. photographer
16. electrician
17. businessman
18. architect
19. dressmaker
20. architect
21. painter
22. hairdresser
23. gardener
24. lawyer
25. baby-sitter
26. singer
27. waiter
28. fisherman
29. mason
30. air hostess
31. taxi driver
32. barman

UNIT 11

ESOL CLASS - SAN PEDRO SULA

INTRODUCTION

In this unit, you will practice the present continuous tense. Later, you will practice reading 'two-syllable' words.

Later, you will work with root words, prefixes, and suffixes as well as words with special vowel combinations and special sounds or endings.

You will also learn some multi-syllable words and finally, you will continue to practice reading and writing sentences as well as reading Bible scriptures.

OBJECTIVES

- Practice the present and past continuous tenses, the simple present and simple past tense of the verbs.
- Practice the use of vocabulary lists about every day activities, recess activities, and action verbs.
- Talk about the weather and the seasons of the year, days of the week, and months of the year.
- Use frequency expressions and conjunctions.

Lesson 119

I AM CLEANING THE HOUSE

119.0 AFFIRMATIVE

The present continuous tense is used in the following cases:

Actions taking place now
a) What are you doing right now?
b) I'm drinking milk.

a) What are you doing?
b) I'm combing my hair.

⟩ show that something is happening now

Future plans – Near future
a) What are you doing tomorrow?
b) I'm cleaning my room.
a) What are you doing on Monday?
b) I'm driving to work.

⟩ show that something is happening soon

Longer actions in progress
a) What are you studying?
b) I'm studying to become a doctor.

⟩ show longer actions that are in progress

1 119.1 ON THE PHONE

Marta: Hi Pedro! This is Marta.
Pedro: Hello Marta. How are you?
Marta: Fine! Are you busy?
Pedro: Well, yes, a little.
Marta: What are you doing?
Pedro: I'm building a sand castle with my son.
Marta: Oh! are you enjoying a time at the beach?
Pedro: Yes. We are having fun!
Marta: Ok. I'll call you tomorrow.

Time Expressions

Present Tense
now
right now
this year
this week

Future Plans
tomorrow
on Monday..
next week

2 WHAT ARE YOU DOING

What are you doing?
I am drinking water.

What are they doing?
They are eating.

WHAT IS HE DOING?

What is he doing?
He is cooking dinner.

What is she doing?
She is playing soccer.

What are we doing?
We are dancing at the party.

What is the cat doing?
It is sleeping.

Everyday Activities

eating pizza
drinking water
cooking dinner
reading a book
studying the lesson
teaching English
singing a song
sleeping
watching TV
listening to music
playing soccer

Sentence structure

I	am	eating	pizza.
You / We / They	are	eating	pizza.

Sentence structure

He / She / It	is	eating	pizza.

4 VERBS I

1. ask   17. cook
2. bake   18. cry
3. bite   19. cut
4. bounce   20. dance
5. brush   21. dig
6. build   22. draw
7. call   23. dream
8. carry   24. drink
9. catch   25. drive
10. clap   26. eat
11. clean   27. float
12. climb   28. fly
13. close   29. fold
14. color   30. follow
15. comb   31. give
16. come   32. go

3 THEY ARE DRAWING

Tomas and Carlos carry a table

They dance Tango

The children play volleyball

babies cry

HE IS CLAPPING

Maria clean the house

Jorge brush his teeth

Rolando play golf

Pablo build a house

Homework: Study the list of verbs.
Write sentences in the present continuous tense.

At Home

Lesson 120

1 ADDING ING

Add ing to the following verbs.

1. run _____	12. talk _____
2. Fill _____	13. tell _____
3. swim _____	14. study _____
4. listen _____	15. sit _____
5. watch _____	16. pet _____
6. cut _____	17. drink _____
7. learn _____	18. eat _____
8. clap _____	19. send _____
9. walk _____	20. take _____
10. stop _____	21. get _____
11. read _____	22. sleep _____

3 Tell what they are doing. Use the present continuous tense.

They / swim

He / walk

They / jog

Marcos / run

If the verb ends in a vowel and a consonant, double the consonant, then add ing.
If the verb ends in a vowel followed by two consonants, only add "ing".

READING   **HOPPING**   **WALKING**

2 WRITE

Tomas drive — What is Tomas doing? He is driving a car.

Andres carry _____

They drink _____

The man fly _____

Eduardo build _____

Omar call _____

They dance _____

Homework: Practice writing sentences in present continuous tense.

135

Lesson 121

THEY ARE NOT WORKING TODAY

1 121.1 THE PRESENT CONTINUOUS TENSE

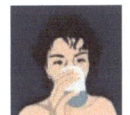
Are you drinking milk?
No. I'm not drinking milk.
What are you drinking?
I'm drinking water.

Are you working?
No. I'm not working.
What are you doing?
I'm resting.

Are they eating fish?
No. They aren't eating fish.
What are they eating?
They are eating chicken.

Is Linda sleeping?
No. She isn't sleeping.
What's she doing?
She's driving her car.

Are the children eating?
No. They aren't eating.
What are doing?
They're studying English.

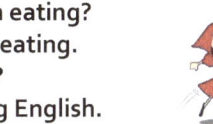
Is the girl studying?
No. She isn't studying.
What's she doing?
She's jumping.

2 VERBS II

1. hit
2. hop
3. juggle
4. jump
5. kick
6. knock
7. laugh
8. lead
9. lift
10. lock
11. look
12. march
13. mix
14. mop
15. open
16. pack
17. paint
18. paste
19. pick
20. plant
21. play
22. point
23. pour
24. pull
25. push
26. put
27. rake
28. read
29. ride
30. row
31. run
32. sail

3 PRACTICE

You
✗ play the guitar
✓ play the piano

Omar
✗ knock a door
✓ eat carrots

Tom and Tanya
✗ ride horses
✓ ride bikes

Ted
✗ jump the fence
✓ read the newspaper

Fredy and Leah
✗ dance Zumba
✓ dance Salsa

Francisco
✗ kick a ball
✓ lift weights

They
✗ run to the store
✓ run to the park

Juan
✗ clean the house
✓ paint the house

the men
✗ opening a box
✓ push a hand truck

Peter
✗ lift a box
✓ pack his things

Mike and Julia
✗ ride a bike
✓ drive a car

Marcela
✗ paste pictures
✓ mix the fruit

the men
✗ plant flowers
✓ march in the parade

the boy
✗ play
✓ ride a horse

4 ON THE PHONE

Ann: Hi Luis! This is Ann.
Luis: Hi Ann. How are you?
Ann: I'm Fine! What about you?
Luis: I'm fine too.
Ann: Are you working?
Luis: No. I'm not. I'm not working this weekend. I'm painting my house.
Ann: Oh. That's good! What color are you using?
Luis: I'm painting it in white.
Ann: That's a nice color.
Luis: Thank you. What are you doing right now? Are you studying for the Exam?
Ann: No. I'm not studying. Well, I'll see you tomorrow.
Luis: See you then. Bye!

Homework:

-Study the list of verbs.
-Write 10 sentences in the present continuous tense in affirmative and negative forms.

Negative Form

I	am not	eating	pizza.
You We They	are not	eating	pizza.

Third Person -Singular

He She It	is not	eating	pizza.

Interrogative Form

Am	I			
Are	you/we/they	eating	pizza	?
Is	he/she/it			

Lesson 122

At Home

1 UNSCRAMBLE
Unscramble the words to form negative sentences in the present continuous tense.

they / driving / truck / are / a / not
_____

not / is / the man / reading / book / a
_____

is / playing / not / Maria / soccer
_____

children / are / the / eating / not
_____

not / boy / studying / is / the
_____

pushing / the man / the / car / not / is
_____

2 WRITING
Write the question for each activity that the people are doing. Answer following the sample given.

Marcela
   Is Marcela juggling?
 ✗ No. She isn't juggling.
   What's she doing?
 ✓ She's jumping the rope.

✗ juggle
✓ jump the rope

Manuel
_____
✗ _____
_____
✓ _____

✗ row a boat
✓ read the newspaper

Andres
_____
✗ _____
✓ _____

✗ pull the cart
✓ push the cart

Angel
_____
✗ _____
✓ _____

✗ drive a car ride
✓ ride a bike

The men
_____
✗ _____
✓ _____

✗ travel by train
✓ sail a boat

Peter
_____
✗ _____
✓ _____

✗ march in a parade
✓ mop the floor

Pedro
_____
✗ _____
✓ _____

✗ pull a box
✓ push a box

Fernando
_____
✗ _____
✓ _____

✗ run a marathon
✓ kick a ball

3 COMPLETE
Complete the *negative* sentences using the present continuous tense of the verb in parentheses.

1. I _____ French in the ESOL Program.   (study)
2. My friend _____ in a factory.   (work)
3. She _____ the house right now.   (clean)
4. The gardener _____ white roses in the garden.   (plant)
5. The boy _____ his wagon.   (pull)
6. The children _____ their presents now.   (open)

Lesson 123

WERE YOU WORKING LAST NIGHT?

1  123.1 THE PAST CONTINUOUS TENSE

Were you walking to the park?
No. We weren't walking to school.
What were you doing?
We were swimming in the pool.

Was the cat eating?
No. It wasn't eating.
What was it doing?
It was sleeping.

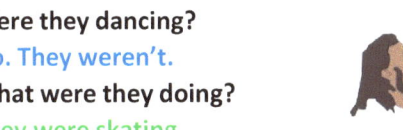
Were they dancing?
No. They weren't.
What were they doing?
They were skating.

Was Luis skating?
No. He wasn't skating.
What was he doing?
He was shouting.

Were the children studying?
No. They weren't.
What were they doing?
They were walking.

Were you singing?
No. I wasn't singing.
What were you doing?
I was throwing a balloon.

2 VERBS III

1. scrub
2. see
3. set
4. sew
5. shout
6. show
7. sing
8. sit
9. skate
10. skip
11. sleep
12. slide
13. sneeze
14. spin
15. stand
16. stop
17. sweep
18. swim
19. swing
20. take
21. talk
22. tell
23. throw
24. tie
25. turn
26. walk
27. wash
28. wave
29. wipe
30. work
31. write
32. yawn

Time Expressions

Past Tense

yesterday	yesterday morning
in the morning	in the morning
at 8:00 a.m.	in the afternoon

3 PRACTICE

 **You**
x play the piano
✓ play the guitar

 **Omar**
x write a report
✓ sneeze

 Suyapa
x talk on the phone
✓ scrub the floor

 **Ted**
x walk to the park
✓ work hard

 **Marcela**
x sing a song
✓ write a report

 **Francisco**
x sit on a couch
✓ sew a shoe

 **Tomas**
x wash the car
✓ sweep the floor

 **Juan**
x work hard
✓ sleep on the sofa

 **they**
x stand by a tree
✓ sit on the chairs

 **Peter**
x wash his hair
✓ wash his hands

 **the boy**
x sing a song
✓ take a shower

 **Tomas**
x work
✓ wave goodbye

 **the men**
x talk to a friend
✓ throw the trash

 **the boy**
x sit by the tree
✓ stand by the tree

4 ON THE PHONE

Omar: Hi Luisa. How are you? I called you this morning.

Luisa: Hi. Oh, yes. I was working and in that moment I was talking to my boss.

Omar: Okay. I was thinking about going to the movies tomorrow. What do you think?

Luisa: Fine! I am not doing anything tomorrow.

Omar: Good! Are you busy now?

Luisa: No. I already finished. I was cleaning the house. What about you?

Omar: A few minutes ago I was writing a Science report. Well, see you tomorrow.

Luisa: See you tomorrow then!

First Person
Aff. I was eating pizza.
Neg. I was not eating pizza
Int. Was I eating Pizza?

Second Person
Aff. You were eating pizza.
Neg. You were not eating pizza
Int. Were you eating Pizza?

Third Person –Singular
Aff. He was eating pizza.
Neg. He was not eating pizza
Int. Was he eating Pizza?

At Home

Lesson 124

1 UNSCRAMBLE
Unscramble the words to form sentences in the past continuous tense.

 They / turning / were / the / to / left
_____

 boy / was / the / swinging / morning / the / in
_____

 was / to / walking / Maria / park / the / ?
_____

 man / was / the / sweeping / floor / the
_____

 showing / was / John / the / to / his / results / boss
_____

 girl / was / ice skating / the / ?
_____

2 WRITING
Write the question for each activity that the people were doing.

Jorge
✗ Was Jorge walking?
  No. He wasn't.
  What was he doing?
✓ He was jumping the rope.

✗ walk
✓ jump the rope

Joe
✗ _____
  _____
  _____
✓ _____

✗ sleep
✓ stand by a tree

Lester
✗ _____
  _____
✓ _____

✗ wash his car
✓ work

The men
✗ _____
  _____
✓ _____

✗ talking on the phone
✓ sing a song

Julio
✗ _____
  _____
✓ _____

✗ walk
✓ work

Mary
✗ _____
  _____
✓ _____

✗ take a shower
✓ talk on the phone

3 COMPLETE
Complete the sentences in the past continuous tense of the verb in parentheses.

1. Juan _____ to Jacob at 8 p.m. last night. (talk)
2. Ana _____ in that office last year. (work)
3. She _____ dinner at 5 pm. (cook)
4. The children _____ at the playground in the morning. (play)
5. The girl _____ a big hamburger at noon. (eat)
6. The boys _____ their favorite movie last night. (watch)
7. _____ you _____ me on the phone in the morning? (call)
8. _____ your mother _____ by the park in the morning? (walk)
9. _____ Maria _____ a shower? (take)

4 TALK ABOUT WHAT YOU AND YOUR RELATIVES WERE DOING YESTERDAY MORNING.

Lesson 125

LET'S TALK ABOUT

1 MY FAMILY PICTURES

Work with a partner. Read the description of each picture. Answer the questions.

This is a selfie of my father. He was having his vacations in Paris. He was having a great time but then it started to rain.

1. Who's he?
2. Where's he?
3. What was he doing?

This is a picture of my mother. She was visiting New York for two weeks. She was standing near the Statue of Liberty.

1. Who's she?
2. Where's she?
3. What was she doing?

🎧 125.1 THE BIG CATCH

One day as Jesus was standing by the lake, and the people were crowding around him and listening to the word of God, he saw two boats left there by the fishermen, who were washing their nets. He sat down and taught the people from the boat.

Jesus asked the fishermen to take the boat into the deep water and put the nets into the deep water to catch some fish. Simon answered: "Master, we were working hard all night and caught nothing."

The fishermen put their nets into the water and they got so many fish that their nets were breaking.

Reference to Luke 5:1-11

Underline the sentences in present or past continuous tenses.

2 MEMORIES

Talk about these pictures. Tell what the people in them were doing.

my friend
Cancun
have fun at the beach

Tom and Diana
at the party
dance

Kenji and Kevin
at the pool
swim

Mauricio
at the zoo
dance

Leonardo
by the lake
ride his bike

Pedro
at the park
show his new car

Asisclo
at the beach
rest on the sand

Sharon
at the ice rink
skate with her friends

3 MY FAMILY PICTURES

Talk about 5 different pictures of you or your family.

Wh Questions...

Who? (person)   **What?** (activity)   **Where?** (place)

THE WEATHER

Lesson 126

1 126.1 **How's the weather today?**

sunny
It's

rainy
It's raining.

snowy
It's

stormy
It's stormy.

cloudy
It's cloudy.

partly cloudy
It's partly cloudy.

clear
It's clear

hailing
It's hailing.

2 **Read and answer.**

Hello! My name is Peter. I am enjoying a very nice vacation in Cancun. I am having a great time! The weather is perfect. It is hot and it is the perfect day to be at the beach.

1) Where is Peter enjoying his vacation?
2) Is Peter having a great time?
3) How is the weather?
4) How is the temperature?

Hello! My name is Ann. I am in Hawaii but I am not enjoying my vacation. I am having a terrible time here. It's raining a lot and it is very cold.. I was having a great time yesterday but today I am feeling so sad because of this bad weather.

1) Where is Ann spending vacation?
2) Is Ann having a great time?
3) How is the weather?
4) How is the temperature?

Hello! My name is Pablo. I am in the Bay Island. I was having a great time at the beach yesterday but today it is hailing. I was going to swim all day but now I can't do it. It is a cold day today and I have to stay at the hotel.

1) Where is Pablo spending his vacation?
2) Is Pablo having a great time today?
3) How is the weather?
4) How is the temperature?

Temperature

It's hot.

It's cold.

It's warm.

It's cool.

Aff. It is cold.
Neg. It is not cold.
Int. Is it cold ?

At Home

Lesson 127

1 ARE YOU ENJOYING YOUR VACATION?
Pretend you are having a vacation. describe each of the weather scenes below.

sunny

_____
_____
_____

_____
_____
_____

cloudy

stormy

_____
_____
_____

_____
_____
_____

snowy

 127.1 Reference to Matthew 14:22-32

Jesus' followers were waiting for him in the boat. Jesus was still with the people, asking them to go home. Then, he went to pray. By this time, the boat was already a long way from the shore. Since the wind was blowing against it, the boat was having trouble because the waves were high. The disciples were still waiting for Jesus in the boat when they saw Jesus walking on the water and coming towards them.

They were afraid, thinking it was a ghost. Jesus asked them not to be afraid, so Peter asked Jesus "Lord, if that is really you, let me come to you on the water." Jesus asked him to come and soon, Peter was walking on the water to Jesus.

But while Peter was walking on the water, he noticed that the wind was blowing and he saw the waves. He was afraid and began sinking into the water. He shouted "Lord, save me!" Jesus took Peter's hand and said, "Your faith is small. Why did you doubt?

3 ON THE PHONE

Don: Hi. How are you doing?

Renee: Well, not so good. I am having a bad time at the beach.

Don: Why? What's going on?

Renee: I was enjoying my vacation yesterday, but today, it is raining a lot and I have to stay at the hotel.

Don: Oh, I am so sorry to hear that!

Renee: I am also having some trouble with the food here. I was eating delicious food yesterday but today I don't like the food I am eating at the hotel. I am not feeling so well either.

Don: I see you are really having a bad time!

Renee: Yes. I am not enjoying my vacation.

Don: That's terrible!

Lesson 128

Let's talk about ...

🎧 128.1 Severe Weather Conditions

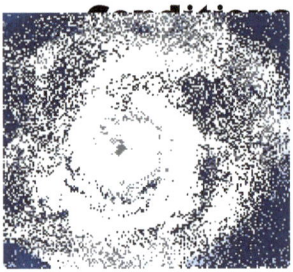

Answer

When did this happened?

What were Jeannette and her family doing those days?

Hurricane Mitch

Hurricane Mitch was the most destructive hurricane of the season in 1998. It was a hurricane category 5.

Jeannette remembers those days...

"I remember those days, it was raining hard. It rained for about 8 days in a row. It was the first time I experienced something like that. There was no school, people could not go to work. My family and I were watching the news all day. We were worried, because many people were losing their houses due to the heavy rain and floods, including one of my aunts who was having serious problems with her house. It was a difficult time but an opportunity to help others. That year I was baptized, and I prayed constantly for my country and all the people affected in Honduras and Nicaragua. The church helped the ones who were losing their houses or furniture. After that, a lady who was helped after loosing her possessions was baptized. She was touched in her heart by seeing how the disciples helped others."

Snowstorms

Snowstorms are common during winter in some states of the United States, especially in the northern area where large amounts of snow can cause serious disruptions in traffic, making every day activities difficult for some people.

Snowstorms can cause car accidents due to slippery roads. They can also reduce the visibility to drivers.

4 🎧 128.2 ON THE PHONE

Kevin: Hi. How are you doing?

Linda: Hi Kevin! I am doing great!

Kevin: Are you enjoying your vacation?

Linda: Yes. A lot! My son and I are having a great time at the island. This is a beautiful place. The weather is nice. The sky is clear, and it is not so hot.

Kevin: That sounds good! What are you doing these days?

Linda: We are eating delicious food and visiting many places here. I am eating a lot and my son Hector is taking many pictures.

Kevin: I see you are really having a great time!

Linda: Yes. We are so happy to be here. We are really enjoying our vacation and we are planning to stay here for three more days.

Kevin: That's awesome!

🎧 128.3 Reference to Mark 4:35-41

That day, at evening, Jesus said to his followers, "Come with me across the lake." So they left the crowd behind and went with Jesus in the boat he was already in. There were also other boats that went with them.

A very bad wind came up on the lake. The waves were coming over the sides and into the boat, and it was almost full of water. Jesus was inside the boat, sleeping with his head on a pillow. The followers were trying to wake him up, saying "Master! Master! We perish. Lord, save us!"

Jesus gave a command to the wind and the water. He said, "Quiet! Be still!" Then the wind stopped, and the lake became calm.

He said to his followers, "Why are you afraid? Where is your faith?" They were very afraid and asked each other, "What kind of man is this? Even the wind and the water obey him!"

Answer:

How's the weather in your country?
What's the weather like today?
What was the weather like yesterday?
What do you do when it rains?

Is it rainy where you live?
How's the temperature?
Is your country a cold place?
What's your favorite weather?

WHAT DO YOU DO ON SUNDAYS?

Lesson 129

The simple present tense is used in the following cases:

To express usual actions or activities
a) I go to work every day.
b) I play soccer on Sundays.

Usual activities may include habits, routines, a daily event or something that happens often.

To express a present time action
a) I study English in the ESOL Program.
b) I work in a factory.

Includes long term activities you do in the present. Even though they are not taking place in the moment of speaking.

For scheduled events in close future
a) My parents arrive at 7 am.
b) The children leave school at 3 pm.

This is often used to talk about transportation.

To express facts or generalizations
a) People love dogs.
b) Children like candies.

This includes to express opinions or believes.

Days of the Week
SUNDAY
MONDAY
TUESDAY
WEDNESDAY
THURSDAY
FRIDAY
SATURDAY

I play golf on Sundays.
I study English on Saturdays.
I clean the house on Mondays.

Time Expressions – Present Tense
every day   every night
every morning   at night
every afternoon   every weekend

1 What do you do?
Practice with a partner.

What do you do at recess time?
I eat a hamburger and a piece of fruit.

Where do you go on vacation?
I go to the beach.

What do they do?
They drive to work.

Where do your friends go on Saturday?
They go to the cinema.

Sentence structure

I / You / We / They	study	English	in the ESOL Program.
Subject	verb	direct object	complement

2 Practice

Where do you go on Sunday mornings?
I / church.

Where do your friends go every morning?
They / gym.

What do they eat for breakfast?
They / waffles.

What do we drink at night?
We / lemonade.

What do they eat for lunch?
They / apples.

What do Ted and Mary drink in the mornings?
They / coffee.

Homework: Practice writing sentences in the simple present tense.

3 Practice
Tell what you do each day of the week.

1. What do you do on Sundays?

   I go to the beach on Sundays.
   On Sundays, I go to the beach.

2. What do you do on Mondays?

   I drive.. on Mondays.
   On Mondays, I..

3. _____on Tuesdays?
   I clean...
   On Tuesdays, I...

4. _____on Wednesdays?
   I cook..
   On Wednesdays, I ...

5. _____on Thursdays?
   I eat...
   On Thursdays, I...

6. _____on Fridays?
   I drink..
   On Fridays, I...

7. _____on Saturdays?
   I come..
   On Saturdays, I...

Answer:
1. What do you do when you are at home?
2. Where do you go to read a book?
3. What do you do when you are happy?
4. What do you do when you are bored?

144

Lesson 130

At Home

1 COMPLETE
Complete the sentences with the right form of the verb in simple present tense.

The children_____hamburgers once a week.

We_____to the beach twice a month.

My friends_____to work every day.

They_____to the gym at night.

Tom and Sue_____by ship across the ocean.

The men_____in a big company.

They_____to church on Sundays.

My friends_____the Bible every day.

The children_____every day in the morning.

2 PRACTICE
Complete the question with a time expression. Then answer the question.

1. What do they do _____?
_____
   clean the house

2. What do we do _____?
_____
   draw pictures

3. What do you do _____?
_____
   drink tea

4. What do they do _____?
_____
   call their mother

5. Do they _____?
_____
   play soccer

6. Do they go _____?
_____
   to the store

7. Do we _____?
_____
   eat chicken

8. Do you _____?
_____
   read a book

Homework:
Write and answer questions in the simple present tense. Describe the activities you do each day of the week.

3 WORD ORDER
Write the words in order to form sentences. Then, write them on the line.

1. water / drink / I / day / every
_____

2. study / every / English / I / weekend
_____

3. buy / store / they / at / Saturday / on / the
_____

4. play / together / the boys / soccer
_____

5. do / their / they / homework / week / every
_____

6. buy / friends / the / Mall / at / my
_____

4 Write the days of the week in order.
1. _____   5. _____
2. _____   6. _____
3. _____   7. _____
4. _____

5 Write questions about daily activities. Interview friends. Write their answers.

Sunday:
_____

Monday:
_____

Tuesday:
_____

Wednesday:
_____

Thursday:
_____

Friday:
_____

Saturday:
_____

6 Tell what your friends do these days.

_____/Sunday
_____
_____
_____

_____/Saturday
_____
_____
_____

Lesson 131

DO YOU STUDY ENGLISH EVERY DAY?

1 SHORT ANSWERS

Do you eat hamburgers every day?
No. I don't.
I eat fruit every day.

Do you brush your teeth in the morning?
Yes. I do.
I brush my teeth three times a day.

Do you have salad for dinner?
Yes. I do.
I eat salad for dinner twice a week.

2 PRACTICE

Do you get home early after work?
× No/come late

Do the boys make their beds every day?
✓ Yes/every morning

Do your friends have pasta for dinner?
× No/chicken

Do your children brush their hair at night?
× No/in the morning

Do you get dressed in the bathroom?
× No/in my bedroom

Do your classmates do their English homework every week?
✓ Yes/always

Sentence structure

Do / Aux.	I you we they	study / verb	a second language? / complement

3 ASK AND ANSWER

1. What do you do every day?
2. What do you on Saturday morning?
3. What do your parents do on Sunday morning?
4. Do you eat vegetables?

4 🎧 131.1 DAILY ROUTINES I

1. wake up
2. wash your face
3. take a shower
4. dry your hair
5. brush your hair
6. eat breakfast
7. brush your teeth
8. get dressed
9. go to the bathroom
10. make your bed
11. go to school
12. study a second language
13. come home
14. get home
15. do your homework
16. have dinner
17. take a bath
18. go to sleep

5 THE SEASONS OF THE YEAR

ANSWER
- How is the spring in your country?
- What do you do in Spring?
- What do your friends do in Summer?
- Do you like Summer? Why or why not?
- How's the weather in Winter?
- What is your favorite season of the year?

HOW ARE THESE SEASONS IN YOUR COUNTRY?

_____   _____   _____

EXPRESSIONS OF FREQUENCY

every day	at noon/midday	once a day, a week, a month, a year
every other day	at night	twice a day, a week, a month, a year
every week	daily	three times a day, a week, a month, a year
every month	weekly	
every year	monthly	
	annually	

HOW ?

is used to ask in what manner, by what means, or in what condition.
It is used to ask about people or objects.

Homework: Practice writing sentences in the simple present tense. Use expressions of frequency.

146

At Home

Lesson 132

1 SHORT ANSWERS
Use frequency expressions to answer.

Do you go to the Mall on Sundays?
No._____
I_____

Does your sisters dry their hair every day?
No._____
She_____

Do you do your English homework on Sunday?
No._____
I_____

2 PRACTICE
Write complete questions. Use short answers. Then, write an affirmative sentence to explain.

you/get home early
× No/get home late
_____
_____
_____

your sons/make their beds
× No/sometimes
_____
_____
_____

Carlos and Martha/have pasta for dinner
× No/chicken
_____
_____
_____

your children/brush their hair
× No/in the morning
_____
_____
_____

you/brush your teeth once a day
× No/three times a day
_____
_____
_____

The girls/study English on Sundays
× No/On Saturdays
_____
_____
_____

The girls/go to the beach every weekend
× No/once a month
_____
_____
_____

3 DAILY ROUTINES
Write about each person's daily routines.

Peter_____ early every morning. Then he_____, and_____. After that Peter _____ and_____ _____. At night, he_____ _____ and_____.

Julia_____ around 6:00 am. Then, She _____, and _____. After, she_____. Julia_____. Later on, she_____.

I_____
_____
_____
_____
_____

4 THE SEASONS OF THE YEAR
List three seasons of the year.
Describe the activities you do in each season.

_____
_____
_____
_____
_____

_____
_____
_____
_____
_____

_____
_____
_____
_____
_____

Complete the questions. Then, ask your partner.

HOW?

_____do you say "___" in English?
_____do you get to work?
_____do you get in touch with your family?
_____do your feel in hot days?
_____do you celebrate Christmas?

147

Lesson 133

1 MONTHS OF THE YEAR

January	July
February	August
March	September
April	October
May	November
June	December

When is your birthday?
What's your favorite month of the year? Why?
What do you celebrate in December?
When do you celebrate Christmas?
How do you celebrate Christmas?
When do you celebrate Independence Day in your country?

2 DAILY ROUTINES II

1. floss
2. drive to work
3. make coffee
4. take a walk
5. do the laundry
6. do the dishes
7. read the paper
8. clean the house
9. take a nap
10. shave
11. go grocery shopping
12. cook dinner
13. do your make-up
14. do your hair

3 THE SIMPLE PRESENT - NEGATIVE FORM

I DON'T SLEEP IN THE AFTERNOON.

Do you wake up early in the mornings?
Yes. I wake up early from Monday to Friday.
but I don't wake up early on Saturdays.

Do you brush your teeth every day?
Yes. I brush my teeth every morning, but I don't brush my teeth in the afternoon.

Do you eat breakfast every morning?
No. I don't eat breakfast every morning.
I only eat breakfast on the weekends.

? you/get home early after work
× No/get home late

? You/ brush your hair twice a day
× No/once a day

? Martha and Ted /eat salad for lunch
× No/chicken

? the boys/go to bed early at night
× No/very late

? your friends /walk to work
× No/drive

Grammar

Affirmative: They drink coffee in the mornings.
Negative: They don't drink coffee in the mornings.
Interrogative: Do they drink coffee in the mornings?

4 RECESS ACTIVITIES

1. jump rope
2. play tag
3. play leapfrog
4. do summersaults
5. play in the dirt
6. splash in the puddles
7. fight
8. play hide-and-go-seek
9. catch bugs
10. tease children
11. race
12. play on the bars
13. play on the swings
14. do handstands
15. play hopscotch

5 READING PRACTICE

My son usually plays in the yard. He has a lot of fun playing with friends. He plays hides and catches bugs. He likes bugs, so he catches them and takes their pictures. Then, he sets them free but collects the pictures he takes of them.

Francisco and Martha like to go to the playground. They want to go every afternoon to play with their friends. They play on the swings, and also play on the bars for hours. They really enjoy going to the park.

Allan is 10 years old. He likes to have fun. He plays with his best friends every day.

He does summersaults, he plays in the dirt and jumps the rope. He is a very active boy.

DO YOUR CHILDREN PLAY HOPSCOTCH?
DO THEY PLAY IN THE DIRT?
DOES YOUR SON PLAY TAG WITH FRIENDS?
DOES YOUR DAUGHTER PLAY LEAPFROG?
DOES YOUR DAUGHTER JUMP THE ROPE?

CONJUNCTIONS

Are words that connect other words or phrases.
and : joins two words together
or : shows a choice or possibility
but : shows opposite ideas
so : shows the result or effect

WHEN?

is used to ask for the time in which something happened. It refers to how soon, what moment or date.

At Home

Lesson 134

1 SHORT ANSWERS

Find the months of the year. Write them in order.

```
j a n u a r y j d r a g
f u b c p d o u o b p y
e g o e i e h n y a r o
b u a s e c t e t o i c
r s e p t e m b e r l t
u t c n e m a r c h i o
a e u i g b u m a y i b
r e n o v e m b e r g e
y s p l o r t j u l y r
```

1. _____
2. _____
3. _____
4. _____
5. _____
6. _____
7. _____
8. _____
9. _____
10. _____
11. _____
12. _____

Answer the questions.

1. When is your birthday?
   _____
2. What's your favorite month of the year?
   _____
3. What makes that month special for you?
   _____
4. When do you celebrate Christmas?
   _____
5. How do you celebrate Christmas?
   _____

2 RECESS ACTIVITIES

Write complete sentences for the children's favorite recess activities. Then, ask your partner.

	Ann	Mary	Cesi	Lizzi	Peter
1. jump rope	✓				✓
2. play tag			✓		
3. play leapfrog					✓
4. do summersaults	✓	✓		✓	
5. play in the dirt	✓				✓
6. splash in the puddles		✓	✓		
7. fight				✓	
8. play hide-and-go-seek		✓			
9. catch bugs	✓			✓	
10. tease children			✓	✓	
11. race		✓			✓
12. play on the bars				✓	
13. play on the swings					✓
14. do handstands		✓	✓	✓	✓
15. play hopscotch	✓				

Homework: Write sentences with recess activities.

3 DAILY ROUTINES

Write about the people's daily routines.

I wake up early and have breakfast, I_____, and _____. Then, I_____. After that, I _____ _____.In the afternoon, I_____. _____and _____.

I start my day around 5:00 am. I _____ in before I go to work. Then, I_____, and _____. When I leave from work, I_____. and_____ _____. In the evening,_____ and _____

I_____
_____
_____
_____
_____

4 WRITE

Write questions about the children in exercise 2. Answer them on the second line provided.

<u>1. Do all the children jump the rope?</u>
<u>No. Only Ann and Peter jump the rope.</u>

2. _____?
3. _____?
4. _____?
5. _____?
6. _____?
7. _____?
8. _____?
9. _____?
10. _____?

PROJECT: TALK ABOUT PEOPLE'S FAVORITE ACTIVITIES.

Lesson 135

LET'S TALK ABOUT...
Holidays and Celebrations

Easter

Christians celebrate Jesus Christ's resurrection on Easter Sunday. In some countries Easter includes the 'Holy week' celebration and also the Pascua, and usually lasts for a week or longer.

People celebrate in so many different ways around the world. In Brazil, one of the biggest carnivals in the world takes place at Easter.

People in the United States decorate eggs. They usually organize an Easter egg hunt in which the eggs are hidden for people, especially children to search for them.

What do people celebrate in Easter?
_____

How long does the celebration last in some countries?
_____

How do you celebrate Easter in your country?
_____
_____

Christmas
December 25th

Christmas is an international celebration. It is celebrated in different ways in many countries around the world. We celebrate the birth of Jesus Christ. People usually spend Christmas with their family. They decorate a Christmas tree and their houses with lights.

Some people also build "Nativity Scenes" and give each other presents. They generally sing Christmas carols and make Christmas cards for relatives and friends.

What do we celebrate in Christmas?
_____

How do people celebrate Christmas?
_____

How do you celebrate Christmas in your country?
_____
_____
_____

Labor Day

First Monday of September

People in the United States celebrate Labor Day the first Monday of September. In many other countries, it is called "International Worker's Day" and it is celebrated on May 1st.

People celebrate the achievements of workers. In some places they march on the streets to express their opinion or disagreement about any law referring to the rights of workers in their country.

When do people celebrate Labor Day?
_____

What do people celebrate in Labor Day?
_____

What do you do in Labor Day?
_____
_____

November 26th

People in the United States and other countries celebrate Thanksgiving Day. They gather with their family and friends to enjoy a wonderful time together. People always prepare a meal and thank God for the blessings received that year.

When do people celebrate Thanksgiving Day?
_____

What do people do in Thanksgiving Day?
_____

How do you celebrate Thanksgiving Day?
_____
_____
_____

Talk about it...
What is your favorite holiday? What do you do in that holiday?
_____

135.1 Reference to John 2:1-11

There was a wedding in Galilee and Jesus and his followers were invited. At the wedding, there was not enough wine, so Jesus' mother said to the servants, "Do what he tells you." Jesus asked the servants to fill six large water pots with water. "Now dip out some water and take it to the man in charge of the feast." Jesus said.

Then the man in charge tasted it, but the water had become wine. He did not know where the wine came from. He said to the bridegroom, "People always serve the best wine first. Later, when the guests are drunk, they serve the cheaper wine. But you have saved the best wine until now. This was the first miracle Jesus did in the town of Cana in Galilee.

UNIT 11 SUMMARY

VERBS

1. ask	25. hip	49. push	73. drive
2. bake	26. hop	50. put	74. eat
3. bite	27. juggle	51. rake	75. float
4. bounce	28. jump	52. read	76. fly
5. brush	29. kick	53. ride	77. fold
6. build	30. knock	54. row	78. follow
7. call	31. laugh	55. run	79. give
8. carry	32. lead	56. sail	80. go
9. catch	33. lift	57. scrub	81. sweep
10. clap	34. lock	58. see	82. swim
11. clean	35. look	59. set	83. swing
12. climb	36. march	60. sew	84. take
13. close	37. mix	61. shout	85. talk
14. color	38. mop	62. show	86. tell
15. comb	39. open	63. sing	87. throw
16. come	40. pack	64. sit	88. tie
17. cook	41. paint	65. skate	89. turn
18. cry	42. paste	66. skip	90. walk
19. cut	43. pick	67. sleep	91. wash
20. dance	44. plant	68. slide	92. wave
21. dig	45. play	69. sneeze	93. wipe
22. draw	46. point	70. spin	94. work
23. dream	47. pour	71. stand	95. write
24. drink	48. pull	72. stop	96. yawn

DAILY ROUTINES

1. wake up	17. take a bath
2. wash your face	18. go to sleep
3. take a shower	19. floss
4. dry your hair	20. drive to work
5. brush your hair	21. make coffee
6. eat breakfast	22. take a walk
7. brush your teeth	23. do the laundry
8. get dressed	24. do the dishes
9. go to the bathroom	25. read the paper
10. make your bed	26. clean the house
11. go to school	27. take a nap
12. study a second language	28. shave
13. come home	29. go grocery shopping
14. get home	30. cook dinner
15. do your homework	31. do your make-up
16. have dinner	32. do your hair

RECESS ACTIVITIES

1. jump rope	9. catch bugs
2. play tag	10. tease children
3. play leapfrog	11. race
4. do summersaults	12. play on the bars
5. play in the dirt	13. play on the swings
6. splash in the puddles	14. do handstands
7. fight	15. play hopscotch
8. play hide-and-go-seek	

THE WEATHER

sunny, partly cloudy
rainy, clear
snowy, stormy
cloudy, hailing
warm, cold/hot

SEASONS

Spring, Summer, Fall, Winter

DAYS OF THE WEEK

Sunday, Thursday
Monday, Friday
Tuesday, Saturday
Wednesday

MONTHS OF THE YEAR

January, July
February, August
March, September
April, October
May, November
June, December

CONJUNCTIONS

and, or
but, so

ACTIVITIES

eat**ing** pizza
drink**ing** water
cook**ing** dinner
read**ing** a book
study**ing** the lesson
teach**ing** English
sing**ing** a song
sleep**ing**
watch**ing** TV
listen**ing** to music
play**ing** soccer
play**ing** the piano

TIME EXPRESSIONS

now / right now
tomorrow
on Monday
next week
next month

PAST TENSE
yesterday
in the morning
at 7:00 am.
at 5:00 pm.
yesterday morning
in the afternoon
at night

PRESENT CONTINUOUS TENSE

Aff.	I	am	eating	pizza.
Neg.	I	am not	eating	pizza
Int.	Am	I	eating	Pizza?

you/we/they

Aff.	You	are	eating	pizza.
Neg.	You	are not	eating	pizza
Int.	Are	you	eating	Pizza?

He/She/It

Aff.	He	is	eating	pizza.
Neg.	He	is not	eating	pizza
Int.	Is	he	eating	Pizza?

PAST CONTINUOUS TENSE

Aff.	I	was	eating	pizza.
Neg.	I	was not	eating	pizza
Int.	Was	I	eating	Pizza?

you/we/they

Aff.	You	were	eating	pizza.
Neg.	You	were not	eating	pizza
Int.	Were	you	eating	Pizza?

He/She/It

Aff.	He	was	eating	pizza.
Neg.	He	was not	eating	pizza
Int.	Was	he	eating	Pizza?

THE SIMPLE PRESENT TENSE

I/We/You/They

Aff.	They drink tea at night.
Neg.	They don't drink tea at night.
Int.	Do they drink tea at night?

THIRD PERSON

He/She/It

Aff.	He drinks tea at night.
Neg.	He doesn't drink tea at night.
Int.	Does he drink tea at night?

EXPRESSIONS OF FREQUENCY

every day
every other day
every week
every month
every year
at noon/midday
at night
daily
weekly
monthly
annually

once a day
once a week
once a month
once a year
twice a day
twice a week
three times a day
three times a week
three times a month,
three times a year

WH QUESTIONS

What?   Where?   Why?
Who?   When?

UNIT 12

ESOL CLASS - SAN PEDRO SULA

INTRODUCTION

In this unit, you will practice the simple present tense of different verbs, as well as short answers.

You will use frequency adverbs in affirmative, and negative sentences as well as in questions and will also make questions with 'how often'.

Later, you will learn about different places to live and the parts of the house as well as furniture and appliances for each room, the verb there to be in affirmative, negative and interrogative forms.

Finally, you will use the verb to have in present and past tenses. Through the unit, you will find several Bible Scriptures and Bible stories related to the different topics.

OBJECTIVES

- Practice the simple present tense of different verbs.
- Practice short answers.
- Use frequency adverbs correctly.
- Make questions with how often.
- Learn vocabulary of places to live and the house, including furniture and appliances of each room in the house.
- Use the verbs there to be and to have.
- Learn different Bible stories related to the topics.

Lesson 136

1. THIRD PERSON SINGULAR

Fernando plays catch.
He plays baseball every weekend.

Marcela listens to music.
She listens to Christian music every day.

Pablo plays sports.
He plays Tennis and soccer.

Susan plays cards.
She plays cards with her friends.

2.  136.2 RECESS ACTIVITIES II

1. talk to friends
2. just walk around
3. play catch
4. tell secrets
5. tell jokes
6. read books
7. play dodge ball
8. play games
9. play cards
10. listen to music
11. hang out
12. email friends
13. bully kids
14. play sports
15. show off
16. play sports

Oral Practice

✓ Angel reads books every day.
✗ He doesn't read magazines.

✓ Marie sends emails to her friends.
✗ She doesn't send emails to strangers.

✓ Pablo plays games with his brothers.
✗ He doesn't play games every day.

✓ Mario plays sports on Sundays.
✗ He doesn't play sports on Mondays.

3. NEGATIVE FORM

Fernando plays catch every weekend.
He doesn't play catch every day.

Marcela listens to Christian music.
She doesn't listen to rock music.

Pablo plays tennis and soccer with his friends.
He doesn't play basketball with his friends.

Susan plays cards with her friends.
She doesn't play cards every day.

4. SHORT ANSWERS

TOP SECRET
Does Fredy tell secrets to his parents?
No. He doesn't.
Does Fredy tell secrets to his friends?
Yes. He does.

Does Pablo walk around his neighborhood?
No. He doesn't.
Does Pablo walk around his house?
Yes. He does.

Oral Practice

 John
✗ send emails
✓ send text messages

 Timothy
✗ read fiction books
✓ read Science Books

 Nancy
✗ bully kids
✓ help kids

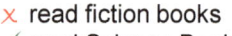 Kiara
✗ read the Bible
✓ read magazines

 grandpa
✗ tell old stories
✓ tell jokes

5. Does he work on Sundays?

Does Carlos work a lot?
Yes. He works a lot, but he doesn't work every day.
He only works five days a week.

Does Mercedes study every day?
No. Mercedes doesn't study every day.
She only studies three or four days a week.

Does your dog take a bath often?
Yes. He takes a bath every two days.
He doesn't take a bath every day.

Grammar

Affirmative: She drinks coffee in the mornings.
Negative: She doesn't drink coffee in the mornings.
Interrogative: Does she drink coffee in the mornings?

Oral Practice

? Tomas / swim in the lake
✗ No. / swim in a pool

? your child / like pancakes
✗ No. / like pizza

? Juana / run every morning
✗ No. / twice a week

? Pablo / watch tv.
✗ No. / read the newspaper

? your son / play tennis
✗ No. / play soccer

Homework: Write sentences in the simple present tense-affirmative, negative and interrogative forms.

At Home

Lesson 137

1 WRITE
Write the months of the year in order.

1. _____ 7. _____
2. _____ 8. _____
3. _____ 9. _____
4. _____ 10. _____
5. _____ 11. _____
6. _____ 12. _____

2 ANSWER
Answer the questions. Use complete answers.

1. What does your best friend do in the afternoons?
_____
2. What does your son/daughter like to do best?
_____
3. What does your son eat for breakfast?
_____
4. Does your wife/husband work at home?
_____
5. Does your neighbor play sports?
_____

3 RECESS ACTIVITIES
Write complete sentences for the children's favorite recess activities. Then, ask your partner.

	Ann	Mary	Cesi	Lizzi	Peter
1. talk to friends	✓				
2. just walk around	✓		✓		
3. play catch				✓	
4. tell secrets	✓	✓		✓	✓
5. read books	✓				✓
6. play dodge ball			✓		
7. play games			✓		
8. play cards		✓			
9. listen to music	✓			✓	
10. hang out			✓	✓	
11. email friends		✓			✓
12. bully kids				✓	
13. play sports					✓
14. tell jokes		✓	✓	✓	
15. show off	✓				

4 WORK IN PAIRS. ASK EACH OTHER ABOUT YOUR DAILY ACTIVITIES.

5 COMPLETE EACH EXERCISE.
Write about their daily routine.

Peter _____ before he goes to school. Then, he _____, _____ and _____. Later, he gets home and _____ _____.

What does Ben do in recess time?

Ben _____
_____

He also _____
_____.

6 Unscramble the words to form sentences. Write the sentences on the line.

1. Does / by / not / train / Tommy / travel.
_____
2. Does / parents / visit / often / her / Martha/ ?
_____
3. Jen / go / does / to / not / the Mall / Sundays / on
_____
4. Indira / Bible / read / her / day / every / does / ?
_____
5. Does / work / Oscar / a / company / in / big / ?
_____
6. not / Ted / tell / to / his / jokes / does / friends.
_____

7 WRITE
Write questions about the children in exercise 2. Answer them using time expressions.

1. Does Ann talk to friends?
Yes. She talks to friends every day.

2. _____?
_____
3. _____?
_____
4. _____?
_____
5. _____?
_____
6. _____?
_____
7. _____?
_____
8. _____?
_____
8. _____?

PROJECT: TALK ABOUT FAMOUS PEOPLE'S ROUTINES OR DAILY ACTIVITIES.

Lesson 138

1 Adverbs of Frequency

Adverbs of frequency show how often something is done.

100%	Always	I always drive to work.
90%	Usually	I usually make coffee in the mornings.
80%	Normally/Generally	I normally take a walk on Saturday mornings.
70%	Often/Frequently	I often take a nap after lunch time.
50%	Sometimes	I sometimes read the paper in the morning.
30%	Occasionally	I occasionally go grocery shopping with my family.
10%	Seldom	I seldom cook dinner early.
5%	Rarely/Hardly ever	I rarely do the dishes after meals.
0%	Never	I never floss in the mornings.

Do you always make coffee in the morning?
No. I don't.
I usually make coffee in the afternoons, not in the mornings.

Do you usually go grocery shopping with your family?
No. I don't.
I rarely go grocery shopping with my family.

Third Person Singular

Does Martin usually take a nap after lunch?
Yes. He does.
He usually takes a nap every day after lunch time.

Does your father often take a walk in the mornings?
No. He doesn't.
He never takes a walk in the mornings.
He always watches tv.

Sentence structure – Third Person Singular

| Does | he / she / it | always | take | a nap | in the afternoon? |
| Auxiliary | | frequency adverb | verb | direct object | complement |

Sentence structure – Interrogative Form

| Do | I / you / we / they | always | take | a nap | in the afternoon? |
| Auxiliary | | frequency adverb | verb | direct object | complement |

2 Practice
Work in pairs. Use the information provided to ask and answer the questions.

your friend/always enjoy his vacation in Hawaii?
(90%) enjoy vacation at home

your mother/usually send letters to her friends?
(70%) send emails

your sister/normally teach English?
(10%) teach French

you/often meet with friends?
(80%) meet with classmates

your father/always leave late from work?
(50%) leave early

Francisco/usually lose his keys?
(70%) lose his keys.

Marilyn/rarely forget things?
(100%) forget things

Andres/often prepare the dinner?
(90%) prepare lunch

3 Verbs IV

1. arrive
2. answer
3. break
4. bring
5. buy
6. behave
7. download
8. dive
9. enjoy
10. feed
11. feel
12. forget
13. hurt
14. leave
15. lose
16. make
17. meet
18. say
19. see
20. send
21. speak
22. teach
23. understand
24. wear
25. bite
26. hit
27. lie
28. prepare
29. sell
30. imitate

An adverb of frequency goes after the verb To Be:
I am always busy on Sundays.

An adverb of frequency goes before other verbs:
I usually bring my dictionary to class.

4 How often..?

How often do you send cards to your friends?
I always send birthday cards.
I sometimes send invitation cards too.
How often do your neighbors feed their pets?
They usually feed their pets two times a day.
How often does Carmen download music?
They rarely feed their cats three times a day.
She sometimes downloads music.
She almost never buys a CD.
How often does Felipe wear jeans?
He rarely wears jeans.
She generally wears formal pants.

5 Practice
Work in pairs. Make questions with how often. Answer using the information provided.

Rolando buy fast food?
(5%) / buy salads
He rarely buys fast food. He usually buys salads.

The boy break a dish?
(50%) / break a toy

Francisco feel happy?
(70%) / feel sad

Marilyn sell clothes?
(100%) / sell shoes

Andres buy apples?
(90%) / buy bananas

David download music?
(70%) / download videos

Mark speak Spanish?
(30%) / speak English

Javier lose his wallet?
(80%) / lose his keys.

Marie read Magazines?
(10%) / read books

Mirna send letters?
(5%) / text messages

Xavier feed the dog?
(0%) / feed the rabbit

At Home

Lesson 139

1 ADVERBS OF FREQUENCY
Add the correct frequency adverb to each sentence.

- 90% I exercise in the mornings.
- 50% I drink orange juice at breakfast.
- 5% I walk my dog in the evening.
- 80% I watch the news at night.
- 70% I forget my keys at home.
- 10% I cook dinner on Sundays.
- 30% I read the newspaper.
- 0% I say rude words to people.
- 100% I enjoy being with friends.

2 WRITE
Unscramble the questions. Write them on the first line. Then, answer them using the right frequency adverb.

1. does / always / Marvin / music / download / ?
_____
No. _____
(50%)

2. Ted / does / usually / his nails / bite / ?
_____
No. _____
(100%)

3. do / always / you / the / t.v./ evening/ in / watch / ?
_____
No. _____
(30%)

4. does / usually / Tom / to do / forget / homework/ ?
_____
No. _____
(10%)

5. Carla / normally / to work / wear / does / jeans / ?
_____
No. _____
(0%)

6. French/ normally / you / do / at school / teach / ?
_____
Yes. _____
(80%)

7. always / your / does / son / behave / school /at/?
_____
No. _____
(70%)

Homework: Write questions in the simple present tense –third person. Then, answer them.

3 word search
Find the 12 verbs hidden. Write the words on the lines provided.

```
a n s w e r u t s i h i t
x i b r i n g t e d b b m
l i e u t f l e a v e s e
m c l n s e a e p y b l e
a o n g a e d i v e i n t
k u f i u l t r o k t l e
e r h y b r e a k d e m p
e n j o y t y x m e s t d
```

1. _____ 7. _____
2. _____ 8. _____
3. _____ 9. _____
4. _____ 10. _____
5. _____ 11. _____
6. _____ 12. _____

4 HOW OFTEN..?
Ask and answer questions with how often. Answer the questions using frequency adverbs.

1. you / speak English in class
   How often do you speak English?
   I usually speak English in class.
   I rarely speak Spanish.

2. your friend / buy shoes

3. your father / forget things

4. your mother / go to the mall

5. the teacher / speak French

6. a dog / bite you

7. a ball / hit you

5 Ask a partner questions with how often.
1. your sister / eat pasta?
2. your best friend / eat pizza?
3. you / go to the movies with friends?
4. your mother / cook dinner

Lesson **140**

1 WHERE DO YOU LIVE?

apartment building
I live in an apartment building.

barn
They live in a barn.

house
She lives in a house.

cabin
We live in a cabin.

mansion
John lives in a mansion.

hut
Sandy lives in a hut.

mobile home
She lives in a mobile home.

cave
Bats live in caves.

castle
The king lives in a castle.

tree house
Roy lives in a tree house.

tent
Sam lives in a tent.

teepee
The man lives in a teepee.

trailer
He lives in a trailer.

igloo
They live in an igloo.

skyscraper
We live in a skyscraper.

THE HOUSE
Vocabulary

 living room
 bedroom
 laundry room
 kitchen
 dining room
 garage
 garden
 attic
 bathroom
 driveway
 roof
 gate
 chimney
 backyard
fence   basement

 city
 town   village

3 VERB THERE TO BE
THERE'S...   **Singular**

Affirmative
- There is a big garage in the house.
- There is a long hallway on the second floor.

Negative
- There isn't a big yard in the house.
- There isn't a nice fence in the yard.

Interrogative
- Is there a garage in the new house?
- Is there a chimney in the house?

Short answers
- Yes, there is / No, there isn't

Choose some of the words to practice asking and answering questions with a partner.

4 CONVERSATION PRACTICE

1. Look at the pictures of the parts of the house. Ask questions about them.

- Where do you live?
I live in an apartment building.

- Where are you?
I am in the bedroom.

- Is there a porch in your house?
Yes, there is. / No, there isn't.

Pair work:
- Is your house big or small?
- Do you live with your parents?
- Do you live in an apartment building?
- Do you live in a big city?
- Is there a driveway where you live?
- Is there a chimney in your house?
- Is there a gate where you live?
- Is there a garden in your house?
- Is there a big living room in your house?
- Is there a basement in your house?
- Is there an attic in your house?
- Is there a pool in your house?

157

Lesson 141

At Home

1 PLACES TO LIVE
Write the question on the first line. Answer it on the second line.

They/live?
_____
_____

You/live?
_____
_____

I/live?
_____
_____

She/live?
_____
_____

He/live?
_____
_____

We/live?
_____
_____

Antonio/live?
_____
_____

2 WORD ORDER
Write the words in order to make questions. Write them on the first line. Then, answer them.

1. does / a cabin / Cindy / live / in / ?
_____
No. _____

2. Teddy / does / a hut / live / in / ?
_____
No. _____

3. there / is / your / garden / house / a / in / ?
_____
No. _____

4. there / is / car / garage / a / the / blue / in / ?
_____
No. _____

5. there / a bathroom / big / is / house / your / in / ?
_____
Yes. _____

6. a / bedroom / his / small / there / bed / is / in?
_____
No. _____

Homework: Writing questions about the house and its parts. Draw a floor plan of your house. Talk about each room.

3 word search
Find the 12 words hidden.
Write the words on the lines provided.

a	t	s	h	e	t	u	t	c	i	t	y	c
c	e	g	o	i	n	r	h	u	t	i	b	a
a	e	e	u	b	a	r	n	a	v	g	s	b
s	p	l	s	s	i	a	e	p	y	l	l	i
t	e	n	e	a	l	d	u	v	i	o	n	n
l	e	c	a	v	e	t	r	o	k	o	l	e
e	r	h	y	b	r	m	a	n	s	i	o	n
s	k	y	s	c	r	a	p	e	r	s	t	d

1. _____ 7. _____
2. _____ 8. _____
3. _____ 9. _____
4. _____ 10. _____
5. _____ 11. _____
6. _____ 12. _____

4 UNSCRAMBLE
Unscramble the words in the box.
Write the correct answer on the line provided

1. morlvnigio _____
2. nbseaemt _____
3. weadirvy _____
4. foro _____
5. nefec _____
6. tgea _____
7. mrgidnooin _____
8. obdeorm _____
9. egrgaa _____
10. ctiat _____
11. dyabcrka _____
12. yemhcni _____
13. ngrdae _____
14. morladunyor _____
15. rmhtaboo _____
16. nktceih _____

5 Ask a partner questions about his or her house.

1. you / live?
2. a garage / your mother's house?
3. two living rooms / your house?
4. chimney / your best friend's house?
5. one bedroom / your house?
6. an attic / your house ?
7. a laundry room / your house?

158

Lesson 142

1 THE LIVING ROOM 142.1

 recliner   armchair  Sofa / couch  shelves  cabinet   plant   lamp   vase stool

 coffee table   end table curtains  fireplace  rug   music system   cushions aquarium

2 TALK ABOUT...

Talk about the living rooms in the pictures.

AFFIRMATIVE
There are three cushions on the sofa.
There are two curtains on the window.

NEGATIVE
There aren't two sofas in the living room.
There aren't two lamps in the living room.
There aren't three rugs in the picture.

INTERROGATIVE
Are there two sofas in the living room?
No. There aren't.
There's only one sofa in the living room.

Are there many cushions on the sofa?
No. There aren't.
There are three cushions on the sofa.

3 INTERVIEW CLASSMATES
Interview your classmates. Make questions using the clues given.

1. windows/the living room
2. tall trees/near your house
3. two chimneys/house
4. doors/apartment building
5. two cars/garage
6. pictures/on the wall
7. bedrooms/house
8. beds/bedroom
9. curtains/living room
10. cushions/on the sofa

4 Oral Practice

1. Work in pairs. Ask your friends about the objects in the classroom.
2. Work in pairs. Ask your friends about the objects in their living room.
3. Describe the house or apartment where you are now living. How many rooms does it have? How big is it? How many people live there?
4. Tell where furniture, appliances, and other things are located in your living room. Use there is/there are and prepositions of place.

THERE ARE
Plural Form

- There are three big windows in the house.
- There are many flowers in the garden.

- There aren't any windows in the house.
- There aren't any chairs in the house.

- Are there any cars in the garage?
- Are there trees in the backyard?

Short answers
- Yes. There are / No. There aren't

There are three cushion...

Matthew 7:24-28

"Whoever hears these teachings of mine and obeys them is like a wise man who built his house on rock.

It rained hard, the floods came, and the winds blew and beat against that house. But it did not fall because it was built on rock."

"Whoever hears these teachings of mine and does not obey them is like a foolish man who built his house on sand.

It rained hard, the floods came, and the winds blew and beat against that house. And it fell with a loud crash."

Homework: Choose two options in exercise two. Present a written report on them.

Lesson 143

At Home

1 NAME EACH ITEM

_____ _____ _____ _____ _____ _____

_____ _____ _____ _____ _____ _____ _____

2 WRITE
Complete the sentences about the objects in these living rooms. Write the missing word or words.

1.

_____ a sofa in the living room.
_____ two lamps in the living room.
_____ three cushions on the sofa.
_____ a chimney in the living room?
_____ a small picture on the wall.
_____ a cat in front of the chimney.

2.

_____ a window in the living room.
_____ two blue armchairs.
_____ three cushions on the sofa.
_____ a music system on the table.
_____ a small picture on the wall.
_____ a tall lamp next to the curtains.

3 Practice
Write affirmative statements about the living room.
1. _____ three cushions on the sofa.
2. _____ a chimney in the living room.
3. _____ two curtains in the living room.

Change the sentences to negative form.
1. _____.
2. _____.
3. _____.

Change the affirmative sentences to questions.
1. _____.
2. _____.
3. _____.

4 What did you learn in Matthew 7:24-29?
_____
_____
_____

5 Write
Describe your living room.
_____
_____
_____
_____
_____
_____

6 Interview People
Ask about their houses. Write questions and answers on the lines.
1. _____
_____
2. _____
_____
3. _____
_____
4. _____

Homework: Practice writing sentences telling the locations of objects.

Lesson 144

MEMORY VERSE

Jesus said to his followers, "There are many rooms in my Father's house. I would not tell you this if it were not true. I am going there to prepare a place for you."

John 14:1-2

Complete the idea

_____ is talking to the _____ about his Father's _____. Jesus _____ going to prepare a _____ for you.

THE FATHER'S HOUSE  144.2

John 14:1-9

Jesus said, "Don't be troubled. Trust in God and trust in me. There are many rooms in my Father's house. I would not tell you this if it were not true. I am going there to prepare a place for you. After I go and prepare a place for you, I will come back. Then, I will take you with me, so that you can be where I am. You know the way to the place where I am going."

Thomas said, "Lord, we don't know where you are going, so how can we know the way?"

Jesus answered, "I am the way, the truth, and the life. The only way to the Father is through me. If you really knew me, you would know my father too. But now you know the Father. You have seen Him."

ANSWER:

- Jesus said, "There are many rooms in my Father's house."
- How do you think the Father's house might be?
- What adjectives could you use to describe it?

1 🎧 144.1 THE BEDROOM

- wardrobe
- closet
- mirror
- rocking chair
- double bed
- cradle
- dresser
- hanger
- bedtime table
- twin bunk bed
- bed
- alarm clock
- fan
- sheet
- blanket
- CD player

3 ROLE PLAY

1. Pretend you left your English book in your bedroom. Call your mother or a relative on the telephone. Tell them where to find the book in your room.
2. Pretend you and your partner are going to buy a house together. Design the house, discussing each room and how it will look.
3. Describe your bedroom. Is it large or small? Nice or ugly? Clean or messy?

2 ORAL PRACTICE

Work in pairs. Ask your classmates about the furniture and objects in their bedrooms.

1.

2.

Is there a beach ball on the floor?
Is there a radio in your room?
Are there two cell phones on the bed?
Is there a big bed in your room?

Is there a window in your room?
Is there a closet in your room?
Are there two chairs in your room?
Are there some books on the shelves?

4 ORAL PRACTICE

Work with a partner. Ask questions about the objects in your bedrooms. Use new vocabulary.

Homework: Pretend that one of these bedrooms is yours and the other one is your friend's bedroom. Describe them.

Lesson 145

At Home

1 NAME EACH ITEM

     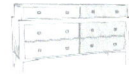

_____ _____ _____ _____ _____ _____ _____

_____ _____ _____ _____ _____ _____ _____

2 PAIR WORK

Complete the sentences or questions about their bedrooms. Talk about the children's bedrooms.

1.   Hello! I am Ann. This is my bedroom.

_____ a hanger in the bedroom?
_____ any books on the bookshelf?
_____ two soccer balls on the floor.
_____ two pillows on the bed.
_____ a cell phone on the bed?
_____ a fan in the bedroom.

2.  Hello! I am Peter. This is my bedroom.

_____ a radio in the bedroom.
_____ two armchairs next to the bed.
_____ two lamps in the bedroom?
_____ a rug on the floor?
_____ a fan in the bedroom.
_____ two pillows on the bed.

3 Practice

Talk about the bedrooms in the pictures.
1. _____ two pillows on the bed.
2. _____ a bed in the bedroom.
3. _____ a hanger on the bed.

Change the sentences to negative form.
1. _____.
2. _____.
3. _____.

Change the sentences to questions.
1. _____.
2. _____.
3. _____.

4 What did you learn in John 14:1-9?

_____
_____
_____

5 Write

Describe your bedroom.

_____
_____
_____
_____

6 Write

Write questions about the house and bedroom. Interview family or friends and write their answers.

1. _____
2. _____
3. _____
4. _____

Lesson 146

VERB TO HAVE

I have a big bathroom.
I have a new sink in my bathroom.
My parents have a modern bathroom.
My friends have a nice bathtub in their bathroom.
They have a new juicer and a new tea pot.

SENTENCE STRUCTURE

I / you / we / they	have	a big kitchen.
	verb	complement

THIRD PERSON

Joe has a big kitchen.
Carmen has a new sink in her kitchen.
My mother has a nice microwave in her kitchen.
My friend Sue has a small kitchen.
I like my kitchen. It has everything I need.

SENTENCE STRUCTURE

He / She / It	has	a big kitchen.
	verb	complement

1 PAIR WORK

Talk about the kitchen items that you and your friends have.

2 SHORT ANSWERS

Work in pairs. Practice short answers.

1. Do you have a big kitchen?
   Yes. I do.

2. Do you have an old blender in your kitchen?
   No. I don't.
   I have a new blender in my kitchen.

3. Do your parents have an old style kitchen?
   No. They don't.
   My parents have a modern kitchen.

4. Do your friends have a new stove?
   Yes. They do.
   My friends have a new stove in their kitchen.

5. Does Carmen have a small kitchen?
   Yes. She does.
   Carmen has a very small kitchen.

SENTENCE STRUCTURE

Do	I / you / we / they	have	a big kitchen	?
Auxiliary		verb	complement	

THIRD PERSON SINGULAR

Does	he / she / it	have	a big kitchen	?
Auxiliary		verb	complement	

THE KITCHEN

peeler, plate, fork, cutting board, cup
knife, spoon, juicer, glass, frying pan
blender, salt shaker, pot, mug, coffee maker
stove, grater, kettle, jar, bowl
kitchen mitten, apron, paper towel, dish towel, tea kettle
fridge, stove, toaster, microwave, dishes

3 PRACTICE

Work in pairs.
Ask to each other.

you/blender
✗ No._____
Your mother/new toaster
✗ No._____
best friend/big oven
✗ No._____
Carol/microwave
✓ Yes._____
Jorge/orange bowls
✗ No._____
Mary/silver spoons
✓ Yes._____
Ted/many dishes
✓ Yes._____
Silvia Cruz/paper towel
✓ Yes._____
Maria Guevara/tea kettle
✗ No._____
Deysi/new dishes
✗ No._____

4 AT THE KITCHEN STORE

Read the dialogue in pairs.

Clark: Hello. Welcome to the Kitchen Store. How can I help you?

Ana: Hello. I just moved to my new house and I have to buy some kitchen utensils.

Clark: Great! We have all kinds of kitchen utensils and the best prices.

Ana: Good. I need a small blender, a toaster, a medium size microwave and a set of kitchen knives.

Clark: Here they are. We have everything you need right here. Is there anything else you need?

Ana: Let's see.. yes, give me please a set of spoons and .. Oh! and a small coffee maker too.

Clark: I'm sorry! We don't have small ones, but we have this modern medium size coffee maker.

Ana: Oh, this is just fine. Thank you so much.

Clark: You're welcome.

Lesson 147

At Home

1 Name each item

_____ _____ _____ _____ _____ _____ _____

_____ _____ _____ _____ _____ _____ _____

2 write
Complete the questions about the objects in your kitchen. Write short answers to each question.

_____ fridge in the kitchen? _____
_____ a kitchen cabinet? _____
_____ a blender in your kitchen? _____
_____ a tea kettle in your kitchen? _____
_____ a microwave in your kitchen? _____

3 Word order
Write the words in order to form sentences.

1. have / they / oven / a / their / big / kitchen / in
_____
2. a / has / Mary / her / microwave / in / kitchen
_____
3. Rigo / fridge / his / in / a / has / kitchen / new
_____
4. has / kitchen / house / big / her / a / in / Rosa
_____
5. have / juicer / a / nice / your / in / kitchen / you
_____
6. has / she / blender / toaster / and / a / a
_____
7. Ted and Mia / kitchen / a / their / house / big / have / in
_____
8. has / oven / big / her / a / kitchen / teacher / the / in
_____

4 Change sentences 1-6 from exercise 3 to questions.

1. _____
2. _____
3. _____
4. _____
5. _____
6. _____

5 Describe your kitchen.

_____
_____
_____
_____
_____
_____

6 Unscramble
Unscramble the words.
Write the correct answer on the line.

1. gum _____
2. rcijue _____
3. lobw _____
4. raj _____
5. letkte _____
6. retarg _____
7. voste _____
8. fneik _____
9. nopos _____
10. rfok _____
11. taple _____
12. sdehis _____
13. rtaoset _____

148.1 THE BATHROOM

Lesson 148

- comb
- brush
- washbasin
- toothbrush
- first aid kit
- lotion
- soap
- sponge
- toothpaste
- hair dryer
- dental floss
- bathtub
- bath toys
- tap/faucet
- toilet paper
- mouthwash
- toilet
- razor
- scale
- shower

1 NEGATIVE FORM

I don't have a big bathroom.
I don't have a new sink in my bathroom.
My friends don't have a modern bathroom.
They don't have a bathtub.

SENTENCE STRUCTURE

I / you / we / they	don't	have	a big bathroom.
	negative	verb	complement

2 SHORT ANSWERS
Practice questions and short answers.

Asisclo and Kevin/big house?
No./small house

Your friends/bathtub?
No./shower

Your parents/two bathrooms?
No./only one

The children/a new toilet?
No./old toilet

DOES HE HAVE A NEW SHOWER?

Does he have a shower in his bathroom?
No. He doesn't.

Does she have a trash bin in her bathroom?
Yes. She does.

Does the cat have a bathroom?
Yes. It does.
It has its own bathroom.

3 148.2 AT THE MALL
Read the dialogue.

Marie: Hi my friend. How are you doing?

Sue: Hi. I'm doing great! What about you?

Marie: I am purchasing some things for my new bathroom.

Sue: Oh, that's good. I imagine you have a lot of shopping to do.

Marie: Yes. I have to buy a towel rack and a new set of towels. I also have to buy a new toaster and a set of knives.

Sue: There's a good store where you can find all you need here at the mall. Last week I bought a bathtub and a new toilet there.

Marie: You mean The House Store.

Sue: Yes. Well, I hope you find all you need. See you later.

Marie: Bye. See you!

4 THIRD PERSON

Joe doesn't have a big bathtub.
Carol doesn't have a new shower.
My mother doesn't have a lotion.
My friend Sue doesn't have a brush.

SENTENCE STRUCTURE

He / She / It	doesn't	have	a toothpaste.
	negative	verb	complement

5 PAIR WORK

1. Make complete questions and answer them.

Claudia/a bathroom in the attic?
No./in her bedroom

Silvia/new toothpaste?
No./an old toothpaste

Margarita/nice sponge?
Yes./a very nice sponge

Lilian/big first aid kit?
No./a small first aid kit

Francis/blue brush?
No./a white brush

Your sister/black comb?
No./a pink comb

Your friend/nice lotion?
Yes./a very nice lotion

Carola/new hair dryer?
No./an old hair dryer

Your brother/razor?
No./a dental floss

2. Describe Carla's bathroom.

3. Ask your classmates about the bathroom items they have in their bathrooms.

4. Ask and answer.

You/bicycle   Your son/toy train
Your/party   You/car
Sandy/new job   Kelly/special dinner
Sam/friends   Hugo/new job

165

Lesson 149

At Home

1 NAME EACH ITEM

_____ _____ _____ _____ _____ _____

_____ _____ _____ _____ _____ _____

2 WRITE
Complete the negative sentences about the bathroom in the picture.

_____ a scale in my bathroom.
_____ a sponge in my bathroom.
_____ a first aid kit.
_____ bath toys in my bathroom.
_____ a washbasin.

5 WRITE
Describe your bathroom.

_____
_____
_____
_____
_____

3 Circle the correct answer.

1. I (don't/doesn't) have a scale in my bathroom.
2. The children (don't/doesn't) have bath toys.
3. They (don't/doesn't) have new toothbrushes.
4. The girl (don't/doesn't) have her own bathroom.
5. Maria (doesn't/don't) have a bathroom in her room.
6. I (doesn't/don't) have two bathrooms in my house.
7. Victor (doesn't/don't) have a new toilet in his bathroom.
8. He (don't/doesn't) have bath toys.

4 Word order
Write the words in order to form sentences.

1. have / they / a new / in / their / bathroom / toothpaste / don't
_____
2. a / hairdryer / Mary / have / doesn't / new
_____
3. Allan / bathroom / bathtub / in / a / have / his / doesn't
_____
4. Eddy / have / doesn't / house / big / his / a / in / bathroom
_____
5. Ana / have / shower / doesn't / a / her / bathroom / in
_____
6. I / have / don't / toothpaste
_____
7. Chelsea / does / bath toys / bathroom / in / her / have / ?
_____
8. doesn't / Cinthia / shower / have / a
_____

6 Unscramble
Unscramble the words in the box.
Write the correct answer on the line.

1. bmoc _____
2. sbhru _____
3. snwbiaahs _____
4. hotrusbhto _____
5. nltoio _____
6. posa _____
7. gpseon _____
8. spthoaotet _____
9. btauhtb _____
10. tcfuae _____

7 Verb to Have
Write the negative form of the verb to have.

1. I _____ a big bathroom.
2. They _____ a nice house.
3. My friends _____ a new sink.
4. My father _____ a razor.
5. He _____ a new toilet.
6. We _____ a big t.v.
7. She _____ dolls.

Lesson 150

1 PAST TENSE-AFFIRMATIVE

Practice sentences in past tense.
I had a big bathroom in my old house.
I had a big sink in my bathroom last year.
My mother had a hair dryer long ago.
My friends had a scale in their bathroom.

SENTENCE STRUCTURE

| I / you / we / They / He / She / It | had (verb) | a new toilet. (complement) |

PAST TENSE-AFFIRMATIVE

Make sentences in the past using 'had'.
Add a time expression.
Daniel/red bathrobe
Daniel had a red bathrobe last year.
Sue/bath toys
Teresa/a hair dryer
My father/a bathtub
The children/a pet
The boy/his own bathroom
Nancy/a new towel rack
The man/a shaving cream
I/a new bathroom

2 NEGATIVE FORM

Joe didn't have a big sink in his house.
Carmen didn't have a new shower.
My mother didn't have a nice scale.
My friend Sue didn't have a bathtub.

SENTENCE STRUCTURE

| I / you / we / They / He / She / It | didn't (did not) have (negative verb) | a new toilet. (complement) |

PAST TENSE-AFFIRMATIVE

Make complete sentences
in negative form.

Ana/bathrobe
Francisco/big toilet
Teresa/ big family
My father/a good job
The children/many toys
The boy/new bath toys
Father/his own bathroom
The man/a bathtub
I/my own bathroom

3 PAST TENSE-QUESTIONS

Did you have a big bathroom in your old house?
Did you have a new sink in your bathroom ?
Did Carla have a hair dryer two years ago?
Did she have a shower in her bathroom long ago?

SENTENCE STRUCTURE

| Did (Auxiliary) | I / you / we / they | have (verb) | a new toilet? (complement) |

SHORT ANSWERS

Did they have a shower in their bathroom?
No. They didn't.

Did she have a new toilet?
Yes. She did.

Did you have a mirror in your bathroom?
Yes. I did.
I had a big mirror in my bathroom.

PAIR WORK

Make questions in past tense.
Answer them.
Ana/towel rack
Did Ana have a towel rack in her bathroom?
Yes. She did.
Javier/big house
Marie/many friends
The children/many toys
The boy/new bath toys
Angie/homework
your father/red car
The man/a bathtub
You/new sink
I/my own bedroom

4 AGO

Ago refers to a time in the past.
It goes at the end of the phrase.

Did you have a small house **long ago**?
Carmen had a small kitchen **two years ago**.
My father didn't have a razor **a week ago**.
I had a meeting **forty minutes ago**.
My friends had a nice party **a month ago**.

5 WHEN

When is also used to express a certain time in life.
Did you have many toys **when** your were a child?
Did you have many friends **when** you lived there?
Did your mother have a car **when** she was young?
Did Carlos have a pet **when** he was a boy?
Did you eat meat **when** you were sick?

✓ Yes. I did.
✗ No. I didn't

6 A SURVEY...

Read the dialogue.

Ted: Excuse me. Could I ask you some questions?

Sam: What about?

Ted: It is a survey about bathroom items.

Sam: Okay.

Ted: Do you have a big bathroom?

Sam: No. I don't. I have a small bathroom.

Ted: Do you have a bathtub in your bathroom?

Sam: No. I don't. I have a shower now but I had a bathtub long ago.

Ted: I see. What are some of the things you keep in your bathroom?

Sam: Well, I have a small first aid kit in which I have some cotton balls and a bottle of alcohol. I also have a box of aspirins.

Ted: What else do you have?

Sam: I have a bottle of shampoo and a conditioner, a razor and a shaving cream.

Ted: Do you have a bathrobe?

Sam: No. I don't.

Ted: Okay. Thank you so much. Please take this bathrobe as a gift for your help in the survey.

Sam: Oh! Thank you so much.

Ted: You're welcome. Have a nice day.

Sam: You too.

At Home

Lesson 151

1 Write
Write the right form of the verb have in the past tense.

I_____ a scale in my bathroom.
I_____ a sponge in my bathroom.
I_____ a first aid kit two years ago.
I_____ bath toys in my bathroom.
I_____ a big washbasin long ago.
I_____ a bathtub in my bathroom.

2 Word order
Write the words in the correct order to form sentences.
1. had / Jose / in / his / a / bathroom / bath curtain / new
_____
2. a / hairdryer / Mirna / had / months / two / ago
_____
3. Javier / bathroom / bathtub / in / a / have / his / didn't
_____
4. Antonio / have / house / new / his / didn't / two / in / bathrooms
_____
5. They / had / white / in / a / their / bathroom / toilet
_____
6. I / scale / had / a / in / bathroom / main / the
_____
7. Chelsea / had / when / bath toys / was / she / young
_____

3 Practice
a. Circle the correct answer.
1. I (had/didn't) have a scale last year.
2. The children (had/didn't) many bath toys last year.
3. They (had/didn't) have a new mirror in their room.
4. The girl (had/didn't) her own bathroom long ago.
5. Maria (had/didn't) a small bathroom last year.
6. (Does/Did) you have two beds in your bedroom?
7. Marcos (had/didn't) have a big sink in his bathroom.
8. Bill (had/didn't) many bath toys when he was 6.
9. Wendy (had/didn't) a nice teacher at school.

b. Write the correct form of have for each affirmative or negative sentence.
- 1. Tomas_____ a job two months ago.
+ 2. They_____ a flat tire yesterday.
+ 3. The men_____ a job offer last week.
- 4. They_____ a nice vacation last year.
- 5. Juan_____ a test yesterday.
+ 6. He_____ a dinner last night.
+ 7. She_____ a bike when she was a girl.

4 Describe
Describe the items you had in your bathroom two years ago.
_____
_____
_____
_____
_____
_____

5 Write
Interview people. Write their answers in your notebook.

1. Did you have a blue cap long ago?
2. Did you have a fast bike when you were a child?
3. Did you have a teddy bear when you were a child?
4. Did you have many friends at school?
5. Did you have a nice teacher at school?
6. Did you have a best friend as a child?
7. Did you have many toys when you were a child?

6 Complete the sentences
Write the correct form of the verb to have in the past tense.

1. She_____ a big bathroom. Aff.
   She _____ a small bathroom. Neg.
   _____ she _____ a nice bathroom? Int.

2. Walter_____ a nice house. Aff.
   Walter_____ an ugly house. Neg.
   _____ he _____ a big house? Int.

3. Lori_____ two children. Aff.
   Lori_____ many children. Neg.
   _____ she _____ four children? Int.

4. Bill _____ a party yesterday. Aff.
   Bill _____ a dinner yesterday. Neg.
   _____ he _____ a great time? Int.

5. Fredy_____ a meeting with his boss. Aff.
   Fredy_____ time to rest. Neg.
   _____ Fredy_____ a good meeting? Int.

168

Lesson 152

LET'S TALK ABOUT...

Igloos

Igloos are small houses made of ice and snow. People called Eskimos live in igloos. Igloos provide shelter and are commonly used only for hunting trips in Alaska. They are usually small to accommodate one person, although some igloos are bigger and can accommodate a group of people.

caves

Caves make a special habitat for different kinds of animals. Bats are commonly found in caves that have access to water. Caves also provide bats a good shelter from predators during the day and also plenty of food. Bats live in colonies. Sometimes the colonies can hold a very large number of bats.

Jesus Heals a Crippled Man

Mark 2:1-12

Jesus was in Capernaum and many people came to see him. **The house** was so full that there was no place to stand, not even outside **the door**. While Jesus **was teaching**, some people brought a paralyzed man to see him. Four men **were carrying** him. But they could not get the man inside to Jesus because **the house** was so full of people. So they went to **the roof** above Jesus and made a hole in it. Then they lowered the mat with the man on it. When Jesus saw how much faith they **had**, he said to the paralyzed man, "Young man, your sins are forgiven."

Some of the teachers of the law **were sitting** there. They saw what Jesus did, and they said to themselves, "Why **does** this man say things like that? What an insult to God! No one but God can forgive sins."

Jesus knew immediately what they **were thinking**. So he said to them, "Why **do you have** these questions in your minds? The Son of Man **has** power on earth to forgive sins. But how can I prove this to you? Maybe you **are thinking** it was easy for me to say to the crippled man, 'Your sins are forgiven.' So Jesus said to the paralyzed man, "I tell you, stand up. Take your mat and go home." Immediately the paralyzed man stood up. He picked up his mat and walked out of the room. Everyone could see him. They were amazed and praised God.

UNIT 12 SUMMARY

PLACES TO LIVE	RECESS ACTIVITIES	RECESS ACTIVITIES		FREQUENCY ADVERBS
apartment building	1. talk to friends	1. arrive	16. make	100% Always
barn	2. just walk around	2. answer	17. meet	90% Usually
house	3. play catch	3. break	18. say	80% Normally / Generally
cabin	4. tell secrets	4. bring	19. see	70% Often / Frequently
mansion	5. tell jokes	5. buy	20. send	50% Sometimes
hut	6. read books	6. behave	21. speak	30% Occasionally
mobile home	7. play dodge ball	7. download	22. teach	10% Seldom
cave	8. play games	8. dive	23. understand	5% Rarely / Hardly ever
castle	9. play cards	9. enjoy	24. wear	0% Never
three house	10. listen to music	10. feed	25. bite	
tent	11. hang out	11. feel	26. hit	**How often..?**
teepee	12. email friends	12. forget	27. lie	How often do you drive your car?
trailer	13. bully kids	13. hurt	28. prepare	I always drive my car.
igloo	14. play sports	14. leave	29. sell	I often drive my car to work.
skyscraper	15. show off	15. lose	30. imitate	

THE HOUSE	THE LIVING ROOM	THE BEDROOM	THE BATHROOM	THE KITCHEN	
living room	recliner	wardrobe	comb	peeler	bowl
laundry room	armchair	closet	brush	plate	kitchen
bedroom	sofa	mirror	washbasin	fork	mitten
dining room	couch	dresser	toothbrush	cutting board	apron
kitchen	shelves	double bed	first aid kit	cup	paper towel
garden	cabinet	cradle	lotion	knife	dish towel
garage	plant	dresser	soap	spoon	tea kettle
bathroom	lamp	hanger	sponge	juicer	fridge
attic	vase	bedtime table	toothpaste	glass	stove
roof	stool	twin bunk bed	hair dryer	frying pan	toaster
driveway	coffee table	bed	dental floss	blender	microwave
chimney	end table	alarm clock	bathtub	salt shaker	dishes
gate	curtains	fan	bath toys	mug	stove
backyard	fireplace	sheet	tap/faucet	coffee maker	grater
fence	rug	blanket	scale	jar	kettle
basement	music system	CD player	mouthwash		
city	cushions		toilet		
town	aquarium		razor		
village			toilet paper		
			shower		

VERB TO HAVE

PRESENT TENSE

I / you / we / they — **have** a big kitchen.
                    verb   complement

He / She / It — **has** a big kitchen.
               verb   complement

I / you / we / they — **don't have** a big sink.
                    negative verb complement

He / She / It — **doesn't have** a big sink.
               negative verb complement

QUESTION

Do I / you / we / they **have** a big sink?
Auxiliary   verb complement

Does He / She / It **have** a big sink?
Auxiliary   verb complement

PAST TENSE

I / He / you / She / we / It / They — **had** a big sink.
                              verb complement

I / He / you / She / we / It / They — **didn't have** a big sink.
                              negative verb complement

VERB THERE TO BE

SINGULAR:
There is a big garage in the house.
There isn't a hallway in the house.
Is there a big kitchen in the house?

PLURAL:
There are some cars in the garage.
There aren't two cushions on the sofa.
Are there some chairs in the living room?

AGO

He had a small house **three years ago**.
She had a nice party **a week ago**.

I didn't have a small kitchen **two years ago**.
Juan didn't have a big kitchen **long ago**.

Did you have a small house **long ago**?

170

www.ingramcontent.com/pod-product-compliance
Lightning Source LLC
Chambersburg PA
CBHW041120300426
44112CB00003B/45